THE PEOPLE'S COMIC BOOK

Red Women's Detachment, Hot on the Trail, and Other Chinese Comics

The People's Comic Book

Red Women's Detachment, Hot on the Trail
and Other Chinese Comics

*Translated from the Chinese
by ENDYMION WILKINSON*

Introduction by GINO NEBIOLO

Translated by Frances Frenaye

Anchor Press
DOUBLEDAY & COMPANY, INC., GARDEN CITY, NEW YORK
1973

The People's Comic Book was first published in book form in Italy under the title *I Fumetti di Mao*. The Anchor Press edition is published by arrangement with Editori Laterza, Bari, Italy.

ANCHOR PRESS EDITION: 1973

ISBN: 0-385-00541-5

Library of Congress Catalog Card Number: 72-76226

CONTENTS

INTRODUCTION

by Gino Nebiolo

My first Chinese comic book came with the tea, on the night train from Hangchow to Shanghai. The girl handed one out, along with the steaming cup, to every passenger. And the recipient balanced the cup between his knees while leafing through the book. The books were small[1] and rectangular in shape, with a jacket in color and the rest in black and white, with one illustration on each of the hundred or more pages. As in the daily papers and many magazines, the wording in the balloons ran horizontally, not vertically, and the story began on the first rather than the last page. This first one to fall into my hands told the true and edifying story of the soldier Hang Chong-tiao. Wounded by the explosion of a cannon that he was tending during army maneuvers, he lost an eye and a hand, but no sooner did he get out of the hospital than he ran to re-enlist.

I noticed that the other passengers, when they had finished their books, made a silent and obviously customary exchange. In this way I obtained a book about a peasant revolt that shook Northern China in the ninth century, at the end of the Tang dynasty. Famine, floods, drought, taxes, landowners and monks who exploited the farm workers, outrageous waste at the imperial court, and elsewhere poverty of the worst kind. After a flood of the Yellow River an intellectual called Huang Chao put himself at the head of thousands of tenant farmers and desperate, landless persons. Huang Chao knew how to ride and use a bow and arrow and had rudimentary notions of the art of war. The poor people's army swelled in numbers, routed the emperor's cavalry in Shantung and his infantry in Honan, finally attacking and occupying the capital, which at that time was Sian in the province of Shensi. But, the text tells us, Huang Chao had no ideological drive. Little by little, he let himself be corrupted by power, failed to carry on the revolution or to effect agrarian reform, and drew away from the common people. Defeated because he could not feed his hungry men, he killed himself with his own sword.

---

[1] At the beginning of each story we have given the size and some other editorial data, which in the originals were on the second or last page. Other data, such as the price and the number of copies printed, are to be found farther on in this introduction.

"The day will come," exclaims an anonymous soldier on the last page, "when we shall all join together under a single banner and the people's justice will triumph over evil."

All through the night we exchanged comic books, without ever speaking. Even the loud-speakers in the corridor, which for hours had transmitted news and patriotic songs, were turned off. The comic books did not tell heroic tales or episodes from history alone; some of them reflected everyday life, particularly in the country. One that fell into my hands was entitled **A Pailful of Manure**, whose peasant heroine, Qien Er-xiao, was, to be sure, a con-scientious worker, but was corroded by the subtle poison of bourgeois selfishness. From her personal latrine she removed a pailful of potential manure for use in her own vegetable garden. Fortunately her husband was a good citizen, ready to give up the manure for the good of the community and, indeed, to scatter it over the collective field. This story was set at a time before the Cultural Revolution, when peasants were allowed to have small plots of land of their own. No law or regulation prevented putting the manure to personal use, only socialist ethics. Around the smelly pail the entire village took part in a doctrinal dispute, and social considerations, quite rightly, won. Qien Er-xiao understood what she was supposed to, happily gave in to her altruistic husband, and thanked the villagers for opening her eyes.

I observed my companions—workers, petty officials, and peasants. The train was moving slowly, at a speed well under the conventional forty miles an hour, and the heating system was out of order. Only two women and one old man laid aside their comic books and fell asleep. Among the others, no one paid attention to the cold or to the repeated stops; they were all completely absorbed in their reading. And if one of them finished his comic book before the others, he looked around him with restrained impatience, and then, when he got the next one, plunged into it without delay. Several times the stewardess came into the compartment with more hot water for the tea, but no one noticed, and the conductor had to knock his ticket puncher against the metal rim of the baggage rack, as if to arouse sleepers, in order to get any attention. At dawn, just a few minutes before arrival at the central station of Shanghai, one of the passengers collected the comics, smoothed frayed corners, and turned them over to the stewardess, who wrapped them in a plastic case.

As a result of this encounter with the Chinese comic book I was led to make certain educational and political observations. First, the stories were forthright and simple, without any elements of escapism or vulgar appeal; second, they aroused an enthusiastic reaction among a public not of young people but of grown-ups, ready to give up their sleep in order to get on with their reading even after a long and tiring working day. Was their sacrifice on behalf of learning or amusement? I had just spent five weeks in Peking and Manchuria, and I had some idea of what today's Chinese think of as diversion. Films, theater, music, and the circus provide ideological shows that leave very little room for what we westerners would call amusing.

Even the opera house of Peking, reformed in 1964 and again, by Mao Ze-dong's wife, in 1966, where revolutionary themes have taken the place of the stories of love and death, of emperors, generals, gods, goblins, mandarins, concubines, brigands, monsters, and clowns of the traditional repertory, and yet are curiously mingled with the single, dancing, acrobatics, and mimicry of classical opera, is now a didactic tool and proud of its ideological function. The heroic railway worker of **The Red Lantern** and the daring young woman in **Girl with the White Hair** exemplify the code of behavior held up to the people, and the people enjoy them at the same time that they accept their teaching. And their acceptance is anything but passive. Queues start forming at the box office of the Peking theaters at six o'clock in the morning and do not break up until night, even though ticket prices are relatively high: one **yuan** (around fifty cents) for the best seats and four to six **mao** (twenty to twenty-five cents) for the rest (the average Peking worker's salary is about sixty **yuan,** or around thirty dollars, a month). The audience follows the drama with a rapt, almost ingenuous attentiveness, quivering with excitement, weeping genuine tears, bursting into sounds of hate at the appearance of the wicked landowner or the enemy military commander, and loudly applauding the long mono-logues of the hero.

The Great World of Shanghai is a group of buildings where seventeen revolutionary theatrical works—including **The Spark on the Prairie, The Surprise Attack on the White Tiger Division,** and **All Together for the Autumn Harvest**—have simultaneous and continuous per-formance. There are also puppet shows, feature and documentary films, and an exhibition hall (with free admission for children) dedicated to the combat against superstition. Here an ex-planation is given of the origin of dreams, to prove that they have no influence over reality; priests, witches, astrologers, diviners, and taboos are mocked; the cosmos is described and a display of the human embryo at various stages, accompanied by recordings, reveals the mys-teries of birth, pregnancy, and conception. The general effect is that of an enormous recreation ground for family groups with simple tastes. Tens of thousands of people go there on weekdays, and on holidays the crowd is so big that theater seats have to be reserved in ad-vance. And yet the shows offered are always the same, so that obviously people return to see them over and over. Even the circus has a political and educational purpose. During the

Cultural Revolution I went to the circus of Wuhan, the steel-mill center of the province of Hopei, on the Blue (Han) River. The public was made up entirely of workers, with tired, unshaven faces, wearing their everyday, worn, cotton working clothes—perhaps the only clothes they had—conspicuously patched and faded from repeated washings. The quotation of a sentence of Mao—"Speaking according to our own desires, we shouldn't want to fight for even an hour, but if circumstances compel us, we shall fight to the bitter end"—was the prelude to a sort of ballet of workers, soldiers and peasants waving red flags. After this came combats between mock dragons, acrobats on trapezes, clowns on stilts or in carts pulled by geese, goats trained to be ropewalkers or to race, with monkey riders, through a hoop of fire, bears on roller skates, trained dogs, horsemen from Mongolia and Sinkiang, and, between numbers, more quotations from Mao, of which the last—"What we must have is a frame of mind both ardent and calm; we must work very hard and in an orderly fashion"—accompanied the final gallop. The onlookers leaped to their feet to sing: "To sail successfully you must trust the man at the helm." Then, unwilling to go away, they spontaneously intoned: "The East is Red . . ." It was after half past nine, and their faces were even more drawn and weary than before. In China, day begins at dawn or even sooner, and weariness comes on early in the evening.

I came upon the comics again in the most unexpected places. I asked for them from news vendors, but they cruise the streets with only daily papers, and newsstands do not exist. I found them, finally, in bookshops, in a few big department stores, and in the schools I was visiting. At the Iron and Steel University of Peking I ran into a group of student-volunteer distributors; I was offered copies by the workers of a cotton mill of Sian; I saw them on loan from circulating communal libraries to peasants, and on sale at factory cafeterias, railway station cafes, bus terminals, soldiers' barracks, and village markets. At Shaoshan, the birthplace of Mao, they are sold by a fruitseller and at Yenan, cradle of the Revolution, by a clerk in the post office.

The price varies from twelve **fen** (around five cents) for a slender, 50-page book, to 35 **fen** (fifteen cents) for a so-called "film-novel." This is not cheap, if we consider that the **Renmin Ribao** costs one **fen** per sheet (this official paper has no set number of pages, and its price depends on the number of them but is never more than four **fen**). A pound of potatoes costs two and a half **fen,** a pound of cabbage five **fen,** a pound of rice twenty **fen,** a pound of pork twenty-five **fen,** a dozen eggs fifty-four **fen,** a three-course meal in a factory cafeteria from twenty to thirty **fen,** and a working family's monthly rent (for two rooms covering a total of 100 square feet) five **yuan,** that is, about $2.50, furniture included.

The number of printed copies is considerable, if we include books produced by the People's Art Institutes of individual provincial capitals, with a purely provincial (rarely national) circulation, and if often a single story is dramatized, designed, and printed in three or four different provinces. I never managed to find out the total number of copies of comic books printed or sold; perhaps not even the Ministry of Industry really knows. The director of the People's Art Institute of Harbin, in the Manchurian province of Heilungkiang, spoke to me of seven million copies distributed over the period of a year to a population of eighty million. The People's Art Institute of Shanghai alone prints sixteen million copies a year, and that of Peking thirty million (including translations into languages spoken in Third World countries). If we look at the comics in the present volume we find that the first edition of **Lei Feng** was of 317,000 copies, which successive editions brought up to two million (it also has the highest price, thirty-five **fen**); the detective story **Hot on the Trail,** published in Shanghai and withdrawn, as we shall see later, during the Cultural Revolution, with its fourth edition reached 450,000 copies (at a price of twenty-four **fen**); **Li Shuangshuang,** 450,000 with its second edition (at thirty-five **fen**); **Letters from the South,** a first edition of 282,500 copies (at twenty **fen**); the first edition of the story of the liberation of the island of Hainan, **Bravery on the Deep Blue Seas,** 200,000 copies in the first edition (twenty **fen**); **San-yuan-li,** a first edition of 190,000 copies and a second of 260,000 (price twelve **fen**), many of which were sold in Hong Kong when relations were tense between China and the Crown Colony in 1967; **Red Women's Detachment,** a total of three editions and 800,000 copies (at a price of thirty **fen**).

Except for a few definite juveniles, there is, in China, no distinction between comic books for adults and those for children. In those aimed at the primary grades the legends contain certain ideograms that are usually difficult to read or have not yet been learned in school, with their phoneme in roman letters beside them. The writing reform, under experiment in the army since 1951 and now introduced into the primary schools, requires students to master first the letters of the Roman alphabet, which make up the phonetic basis of the ideograms; after this comes the teaching of the ideogram corresponding to every group of Roman letters that forms a sound. For example, the word for "rice" is composed of two sounds—**mi-fan**—each of which is equivalent to an ideogram. The student learns to write the sounds of **mi** and of **fan** in Roman letters and then the two corresponding ideograms. In the legends of comics for young children, the phonemes are inserted in such a way that the sounds immediately suggest the meaning of a word diffcult to understand. (The purpose of the reform is to abolish gradually ideograms and romanize writing. Already street and shop signs carry ideograms and

Roman letters together, and the use of the phonetic alphabet and the simplification of ideo-grams have served to reduce illiteracy, which was and still is due to the difficulty of writing and remembering complex ideographic characters. Actually, in the comics neither the legends nor the wording inside the balloons contain many uncommon or difficult words. Novelists are advised to use no more than three thousand words if they wish to be understood; fifteen hundred are sufficient for reading a newspaper, and the comics rarely have a vocabulary of more than a thousand. And in both the primary schools and the schools for illiterate adults, a thousand words are mastered within two years. Thus, two out of three Chinese in the big cities and one out of two or three in the country are able to read the comics, although we must, of course, take into consideration that the density of their reading matter calls for considerable concentration.

This density, by virtue of which the reading matter has an importance and function equal to those of the images (another index to the pedagogical purpose of improving the reader's grammar and vocabulary as well as enhancing his political awareness), is not peculiar to the "little Red comic books" alone; it is part of the Chinese tradition. As the French sinologist Jean Chesneaux has said, something like the modern comics were used as early as the fourteenth century to propagate the teachings of Confucius. And, upon inspection, we see that in the corner of classical paintings there are commentary sentences or verses of the artist, to which have been added those of their admirers and owners, this in spite of the fact that the paintings had no propagandistic purpose but were a cultural product for the benefit of an elite. And with the years, words continued to accompany and explain images; the images were never left to stand alone.

Even in classical times, events of history and everyday life were the chosen themes. In the present volume the story of Viceroy Lin Ze-xu, who destroyed the opium convoys and made war on the English, dates from 1839. The revolutionary moves which the Taipings directed against the imperial troops, as seen from the rebels' point of view, date from 1854. From the same year but from the government viewpoint is an account of the struggle of General Zeng Guo-fan against the Taipings, where the captions are long excerpts from Zeng's harangues to his men, coming out of his mouth in a form that is forerunner of contemporary comics' balloon. In 1901 there were many series on the Boxer Rebellion, showing the "righteous harmony band" attacking Tientsin, setting fire to missionary trains and houses and putting Europeans to flight. Early in the century there was a series on the destructive effects of opium upon the families of the smokers; another on the anachronism of Confucian principles in a developing society (the girl compelled to marry a dead fiance, the son deficient in respect for his father who is drowned in a well by the other members of the family). There was one that must have had an underground circulation because it sympathized with young men who had been thrown into prison for having cut off the pigtails imposed upon them by their Manchu rulers; one that related the exploits of students who broke the law by going to brothels during the period of mourning for the death of the Emperor Kuang Hu; and others about the phenomena of progress—the woman barber of Peking who cleaned her clients' ears, the ladies of Shanghai who used sewing machines, and the young sportsman falling off a bicycle. All these were printed on large sheets, one sheet for each story, or as strips in newspapers.

Around 1920 comics came out in Shanghai with tales of fantasy or else condensations—narrated by both captions and balloons—of fictional and theatrical classics. Ten years later there were the first foreign comics, in the original language and then translated: **Flash Gordon, Mandrake, The Phantom, Mickey Mouse.** They circulated only among the children of merchant families who went to foreign schools, and only in the "concession" cities, where foreigners were in evidence: Shanghai, Tientsin, and Canton along the Pacific, Hankow on the Blue River, and Peking, where there were a number of English, French, and American colleges. Soon specialized publishing houses sprang up; new, original Chinese comics were modeled on the imports and made their way from the coast to the interior of the country.

Imported or domestic, often inspired by the West but with local variations, historical or purely imaginary, the comics were fated to reach ever larger numbers of the population. Even literary men found them worthy of discussion, either condemning their superficiality or else discovering their potential as carriers of culture. Lu Xun, the greatest modern Chinese writer, who was a revolutionary but not a Communist, took an interest in comics, and in 1932 wrote an article in their defense. It was not so much a political analysis as an attempt to strike a balance between aesthetic and social considerations, but in any case the importance of images and their educational function did not escape him.

"Once I had a curious experience," he says. "In the course of a banquet I said that students could learn more from films than from textbooks and that probably a visual method of teaching would one day be adopted. But my words aroused only laughter. Of course, the question is a complex one. We have to consider, first, what kind of films we are talking about. Obviously, American films about how to make money or succeed in marriage have nothing to teach us. . . . Not long ago, in the review **Modern Age,** I read an article by Su Wen, the art critic, condemning the comics from an aesthetic point of view. . . . In the art histories to which we are accustomed we find no reproductions from comic books, and in exhibitions we see only such things as **Rome at Twilight** or **Western Lake at Dusk.** Obviously, comic books are considered too low-brow to belong to such respectable company. But if you visit the Vatican (not having had the pleasure of traveling in Italy, I have seen it only in photographs), you will find that all the marvelous frescoes fundamentally tell stories from the Old Testament and the Acts of the Apostles. When an art historian reproduces one of them under the title **The Creation of Adam** or **The Last Supper,** no one considers it vulgar or propagandistic. And yet the originals are fundamentally cartoons of a propagandistic nature.

"The same thing holds true in the East. After the English had reproduced the wall paintings in the caves of Ajanta in India, they took their place in the history of art. And in China, collectors have for some time attributed value to the **Life of Confucius,** as long as it is a Ming edition. And both the life of Buddha and the anecdotes of Confucius are obviously propagandistic publications, in which pictures are meant to stimulate the reader's interest. When such pictures are numerous enough one can understand the story without reference to the text at all."

When the Communists took over in 1949, they increased the production of comics as an ideological and cultural weapon. They did not do away with the captions and replace them with balloons, which (as Lu Hsun indicated) would have been the quickest way to reach a population at this time from 85 to 90 per cent illiterate. They chose, instead, the type of comics that Umberto Eco calls "verbal conduction," because it compels the reader to pass from the picture to the text and makes for more forceful political communication.

In principle these comics were addressed, as in the West, to the young. Adults had novels in photograph form, something like "movie magazines," reflecting the patriotic and Communist films of the period. One of the most popular of these novels was a humorous narration of the misadventures of a Shanghai policeman: his palaver with old women, the loss and recovery of a multitude of objects, and a tenuous love story. Eventually the comics began to reach an adult public; they became serious and indeed severe, intent upon representing the correct ideology, that is, one in line with the thinking of Mao. Like other cultural expressions, the comics inevitably reflected internal political dissension. Hundreds of series printed between 1960 and 1965, which were influenced, as Chesneaux points out, by the "black" anti-Mao current, were later taken out of circulation. This is what happened to **Hot on the Trail,** the detective story of the present collection, whose "line" is "deviationist." The men who prevent sabotage of the powerhouse of Canton are professionals, not, as they should have been, the rank and file of the Party; the professor, involuntary accomplice of the secret agents, is not described as a dangerous survivor of the old bourgeoisie and his error is all too lightly justified, without any reference to class struggle. In short, the story contains nothing revolutionary, in the Maoist sense of the word; on the contrary, it was considered to have a potentially disruptive and counterrevolutionary effect. Even **Red Women's Detachment,** in the present version, which I was lucky enough to find in Peking during the Cultural Revolution, is out of step with the Maoist line, and the theatrical production that inspired it is now shown only in a revised version. As Chesneaux says, Mao is never quoted and gets no credit for having been the artificer of the Chinese Revolution. In the revised version he is present throughout; the heroine follows his life story, reads the Little Red Book and seeks inspiration for her revolutionary action in a creative interpretation of his thinking.

Just as was the case before the Cultural Revolution, the comics of today are adapted from plays or films, which, in their turn, are taken from novels. In other words, the comics is the end product of an operation carefully thought out in such a way as to achieve a capillary penetration of the masses. It reaches people who find novels hard reading and culturally inaccessible or who live in the isolated two thirds of the country where plays and films are unknown. This may explain the simplicity of the story line, the obviousness of the situations, the pure heroes and black villains, and the lack of any subtlety of characterization.

It may be interesting in this connection to listen to Cun Lin, one of the most active Chinese comics artists, whom I met in the Palace of the Arts in Peking. In keeping with the spirit of Yenan, he maintained that it is not sufficient for a comic story to be understandable by everybody; it must, in addition, win everybody's approval, both for the story and its illustrations.

"I go a lot to the country," he told me. "I work and eat with the peasants. There I find helpful hints for my work; I learn to express myself in forms that the peasants want and understand. Every peasant has something to teach me: how to work with my hands, which is a great spiritual gift, and how to make up stories that tell about it. These peasants suffered under the society of the past and then fought in the Revolution; their lives make up a story that we must retell to them over and over. In order to do the right thing, I try to adapt my drawings to their demands. When they disapprove, I try again. For instance, I took from a novel the story of a young man who, during the War of Liberation, concealed weapons in the house of his landlord until he could turn them over to the Partisans, and himself become one of them. I submitted this story to the peasants of a commune, who approved of the subject but were very critical of certain details of the presentation. The landlord's tunic was too simple, they told me; the **kang** in the poor people's house was too large, the servants were too smiling, and, above all, in the final scene the reader's eye was drawn to the disclosure of the guns rather than to the young man's face. When I reworked the drawings and gave the hero's face greater prominence, the whole thing fell into focus. The people are always right, and it is our job to serve them. And if an artist wants to serve them sincerely, he will defer to their ideological and aesthetic objections. As a matter of fact, the comics with the broadest circulation are by authors who have taken into account the criticism of the masses. I can foretell the success or failure of a given comic by what I know of the author, that is, of his political conscience."

We cannot say, on the basis of this single statement, that such a literal application of Mao's injunction "to serve the people" is the basis of all Chinese comics. But Cun Lin's words throw light on Chinese society, which is little known in the West and which the present volume is trying to reveal in one of its most unpublicized aspects.

The "Red comics" have emerged only sporadically from the country of their origin, and western readers do not know them at all. Having a certain number in hand we decided to present some of them in an organic collection, for the first time outside of China. Our choice is a mixture of stories concerned with everyday life and stories reflecting the Chinese view of history. In the first category are **Li Shuangshuang** (a slice of communal life), **Hot on the Trail** (illustrative of tension and mobilization in a big city), and **Lei Feng**, which gives an idea of the model man held up by Mao as an example to the masses (Lei Fng, who here appears as the Word incarnate, really existed). In the second category are **San-yuan-li** (recounting the first tragic clash between China and the European powers), **Red Women's Detachment**, and **Bravery on the Deep Blue Seas** (two chapters from the War of Liberation, one concerned with Partisans and the other with the regular Army but both with a decisive moment of the epic story of Communist China), and, finally, **Letters from the South**, which shows us how the Chinese view what they call "the war on our doorstep."

The reading of these comics raises a host of questions. There is insufficient information about their specific function (my account is impressionistic and fragmentary, but I doubt that it can be amplified at the present time) and also about the society that engenders and consumes them. . . . The terrain is unexplored, the debate has barely begun, and our book proposes to promote and amplify it.

Translated by Frances Frenaye

EDITOR'S NOTE

The romanization system used throughout this book is Hanyu Pinyin, the official romanization of the People's Republic of China. To facilitate reading for the English-speaking audience, we include below an abbreviated conversion table from Hanyu Pinyin (which probably allows closer approximation to the actual Chinese) to the more familiar Wade-Giles system.

Hanyu Pinyin		Wade-Giles	
b	(bang)	p	(pang)
c	(cai)	ts'	(ts'ai)
ch	(chang)	ch'	(ch'ang)
d	(dao)	t	(tao)
g	(gan)	k	(kan)
j	(jiang)	ch	(chiang)
k	(kang)	k'	(k'ang)
p	(peng)	p'	(p'eng)
q	(qiao)	ch	(ch'iao)
r	(ren)	j	(jen)
t	(ting)	t'	(t'ing)
x	(xia)	hs	(hsia)
z	(zai)	ts	(tsai)
zh	(zhong)	ch	(chung)

SAN-YUAN-LI

Size 12.5 x 10 cm

*Published by Xin-wu Gao,
Hong Kong, 1967*

1. Over a hundred years ago the British imperialists were importing opium into China, poisoning the Chinese people and draining out large sums of money, wildly attempting to ruin our country and destroy our people.

2. The patriotic official Lin Ze-xu went to Canton in January of 1839 to investigate the opium problem. The people of Canton organized into local militia groups to support Lin's movement to stamp out opium. The groups prepared many declarations, songs, and illustrations indicating that they were ready to repulse the British invasion.

3. The British hurriedly handed over twenty thousand boxes of opium. In June all of this opium was burned.

4. The pirates refused to accept defeat and in 1840 launched an armed attack on China. In June of that year they sent a fleet that attacked the Chinese land forces.

5. Lin Ze-xu fortified the approaches to Canton and made defense preparations, as well as announcing that during the period of foreign invasion "everyone could arm themselves and kill the enemy." At this the people rose up, ready to resist the imperialists.

6. The fishermen organized strike forces and, taking advantage of darkness at low tide, launched surprise attacks using fire arrows, explosives, and so on, to set fire to the British ships causing great damage and hardship.

7. Seeing that it would not be easy to take Canton, the British imperialists left to attack Amoy but were driven from there also.

8. The British fleet sailed farther north until it came to the approach to Tientsin. Emperor Dao-guang was extremely frightened; he ordered Lin Ze-xu to be dismissed and ordered the traitor Yishan to Canton to negotiate with the British imperialists.

9. The imperialists demanded that Yishan should immediately demolish all the defense works that Lin Ze-xu had built. When Yishan did as they told him, the British suddenly changed their tune and attacked the Dayu Spit fort with their warships.

10. Emperor Dao-guang sent Yishan to Canton to fight the British, but all the utterly reactionary Yishan could do was to plunder the people's wealth. In March 1841 the British troops approached the suburbs of Canton. On May 22 they attacked Nicheng and Sifang forts, which were key strongpoints in the Canton defenses.

11. The people in the Canton district decided to attack the British warships. Those who could swim went out to the ships to pierce their hulls, thus routing the British pirates.

12. On May 24 some militia under Chen Tang and others entered battle alongside the government troops, killing a senior British officer. In the middle of the following night, Yu Tu-qun of Xin-an district led three groups in a surprise attack, burning and sinking British warships at Chuanbi Yangmian.

13. On May 24 the pirates finally landed at Nicheng, meeting little resistance from the government troops. On the twenty-fifth they occupied Sifang fort from which they bombarded the city of Canton. Yishan in his terror immediately raised the white flag of surrender and opened negotiations for a cease fire.

14. The British troops burned, killed, raped, and looted throughout the city and suburbs of Canton. Over half of the houses in the northwest suburbs were destroyed. Countless women were raped and children killed. The aggressors did not even stop at digging up graves to steal whatever valuable objects had been buried with the coffins, leaving corpses strewn everywhere.

15. When they saw the inhuman behavior of the British, many of the people of Canton began to sharpen old weapons, preparing to fight to the death.

16. The people of San-yuan-li village, on the outskirts of Canton, began to organize themselves at a meeting on the open ground in front of the temple at the north end of the village. They selected Wei Shao-guang as their leader and took the three-starred black flag in the temple as their command flag, ruling that "wherever the flag goes everybody should follow and kill without mercy."

17. Next San-yuan-li contacted neighboring villages and on May 25 representatives from more than 103 villages met at Niulan hill. They decided on strategy and tactics and a huge and determined Anti-British Militia was formed.

18. On the twenty-seventh the traitor Yishan signed the terms of surrender which were posted everywhere, forbidding the people to resist the British pirates. The Anti-British Militia posted their own notices as well, warning the British pirates that they would be utterly wiped out if they continued with their savagery.

19. The Chinese people are always as good as their word. On the twenty-eighth, when the British pirates went to Fatshan to seize women and ships, over 300 militia led by Chen Bi-guang and Su Wen-jing immediately recovered the ships and put the British pirates to ignominious flight.

20. On the evening of the twenty-eighth the British pirates at Guigang fort sallied out to rape and loot. Men of the Anti-British Militia attacked the fort, using small boats, braving the enemy fire. They killed three British officers and killed or wounded several dozen British soldiers, capturing boats, armor, bayonets, and guns.

21. On the twenty-ninth, when the British pirates went to San-yuan-li to make trouble again, seizing oxen and assaulting women, Wei Shao-guang and others killed over ten British devils on the spot, putting the rest to flight.

22. The morning of the thirtieth was greeted with the sound of gongs. The Anti-British Militia, five or six thousand strong, advanced in an imposing array behind the three-starred flag toward the Sifang fort occupied by the British pirates. The weavers, masons, and other workers of Canton also took part.

23. When the head of the British pirates, General Gough, saw the people surging up the hill toward the Sifang fort, carrying knives, spears, hoes, and axes, he was so scared he couldn't even eat his breakfast and, shaking with panic, he ordered the British troops to open fire.

24. The brave fighters of the Anti-British Militia did not waver an instant but pressed forward up the hill. There was nothing Gough could do but leave a small detail of pirates to guard the fort while he himself led the remaining thousand or so troops away from the fort down behind the hill.

25. The Anti-British Militia had guessed that he would retreat toward the northern edge of San-yuan-li. Not realizing that they were falling into an ambush, Gough's troops came hurrying along toward Niulan hill. Just at that moment there was a tremendous beating of gongs and the seven or eight thousand people who had been waiting in ambush charged at the British troops from every side.

26. The Militia's knives came chopping down, spilling out the brains of the British pirates and splashing their blood in every direction. The villagers brought up a locally made cannon and directed it at the pirates, creating even greater carnage. A British ensign named Berkeley was speared and hacked by a villager named Yan Hao-chang.

27. The village women brought tea and food for the Anti-British Militia, setting up a station beside the road to succor the wounded men. Children also joined in, beating gongs and shouting.

28. In the afternoon it suddenly began pouring rain. The British troops' powder was soaked through; their guns became useless and their bayonets were ineffective against the spears of the Chinese peasants, who proceeded to rout the British pirates.

29. At four o'clock Gough hurried back to the Sifang fort and sent two companies to rescue the ambushed troops, but it began to rain even harder and they too were routed by the peasants.

30. The British troops were wearing heavy leather boots which stuck in the mud. Some were killed by the peasants using hoes, others fell to their knees and begged for mercy.

31. That evening it was still raining as the remainder of the British troops, taking their opportunity as the peasants regrouped, tried to escape toward the south. They formed a square and prepared to meet the peasants' attack.

32. The peasants used iron grappling hooks on the end of ropes to throw at the troops, and when one was caught, they pulled on the rope, like catching a big fish. Many of the British pirates lost their lives this way.

33. The fighting went on until late that night. Then the British, taking advantage of the dark, slowly retreated back to the Sifang fort. The peasants were waiting, surrounding the fort, and they killed another two hundred troops and captured ten, as well as a large number of weapons and equipment.

34. All night militiamen roused the population, and from far and wide young fighters came hurrying, to take part in the struggle against the British pirates.

35. The next day before dawn, a crowd of some 100,000 peasants had already gathered at San-yuan-li. This mighty army raised aloft the three-starred flag of the Anti-British Militia and, beating gongs and drums, surged forward to the Sifang fort which they completely surrounded.

36. The British pirates were scared stiff and did not even dare open fire but could only raise a white flag of surrender. But the peasants refused to withdraw and decided to adopt the tactic of starving the British out. There were not many provisions in the fort and as the days passed, the cries of the British could be heard.

37. The British pirates realized that the Manchu Qing dynasty was corrupt and incapable, and so Elliot and Gough wrote to the Prefect of Canton, Xu Bao-chun, threatening him and telling him to think of some way to disband the peasant army.

38. The traitor Prefect Xu Bao-chun had not guessed that the British would be caught in a vise like this; he was just like them in that he feared above all an armed populace, and so he hurried to the Sifang fort and ordered the peasants to disband their army.

39. The peasants took no notice of Xu Bao-chun but were determined to fight British imperialism to the finish. So Xu Bao-chun quickly went to some of the landlords and literati in the Anti-British Militia and threatened them: "If the peasants do not disband, it will be you who will have to pay indemnity to the British."

40. The landlords and the literati, in order to protect their wealth, came round to Xu Bao-chun's side and began to urge the peasants to disband. Because the peasants at the time did not fully understand the true nature of the literati in the Anti-British Militia, they were fooled by them and they angrily began to disperse.

41. In this way the Anti-British Militia was destroyed. But the British pirates did not dare enter Canton again and on June 1 they dejectedly boarded their warships and retreated back beyond the Bogue.

43. The Chinese people kept their word. After the victory of San-yuan-li, the struggle of the Cantonese and of the people of all parts of China against the British continued for a hundred years. Today, just outside the village of San-yuan-li, there stands an imposing monument commemorating the martyrs who fell in the battle of San-yuan-li. Many millions of our people recall the glorious history of our ancestors' struggle against British imperialism; how they refused to give in and in the midst of many difficulties dealt a decisive defeat to the British. Their example gives us great courage for the future, to throw ourselves ever more firmly into the struggle against British imperialism.

42. On the day the British pirates retreated, the Anti-British Militia posted a notice attacking British imperialism's crimes, ending with the firm statement, "We don't rely on the Manchu forces nor do we need government pay. We use our own money and our own strength and if we don't wipe out you pigs and dogs then, we cannot be considered true Chinese!"

RED WOMEN'S DETACHMENT

RED WOMEN'S
DETACHMENT

Written by Liang Xin

Adapted by Sung Yu-jie

Illustrated by Li Zi-shun

Edited by Liaoning Fine Arts Publishing House

Translated and published by the Foreign Languages Press, Peking, 1966

1. It was 1930—the darkest period in Chinese history. The story begins on Hainan Island off the south coast of China's mainland where there lived a despotic landlord known as Nan Ba-tian. He was commander of the defense corps, and he cruelly oppressed the peasants and seized property. The working people groaned under his oppression.

2. Wu Qing-hua, a slave girl in Nan's mansion, was unable to bear the landlord's oppression any longer. So she ran away when the landlord's guards were slack. And all the time she had only one thought in her mind—to escape and join the Red Army to take revenge!

3. As she desperately ran away, she suddenly came face to face with a man on horseback.

4. Qing-hua turned and rushed on. Close after her the landlord's gang, carrying torches and lanterns, ran in hot pursuit.

5. Immediately realizing what it was all about, the man on horseback was filled with anger. "These are Nan Ba-tian's thugs!" his servant said with hatred. Then his master said, "That's Coconut Village ahead, look out!"

6. When they came near Coconut Village, they were surrounded by the landlord's defense corps. "Halt! Where are you from?" The man on horseback dismounted and calmly replied, "My family name is Hong. I'm an overseas Chinese coming back to sacrifice at my ancestral temple."

7. A defense corps leader nicknamed "Gold Teeth" examined Hong's case and found many cards of greeting on top. Searching beneath them he was overjoyed to see it packed with shining silver dollars!

8. Consequently, the master and servant were sent in custody to Nan Ba-tian's dungeon. The girl they had just met on the road was tied to a post. She had been so cruelly beaten that she was covered with wounds. But she was not cowed. "Go on with your beating," she said bravely. "I'll run away as soon as I get another chance!"

9. Before long Gold Teeth brought Lao Si, the landlord's junior steward, and said to him with a servile smile, "They are the new ones. Got pots of money!" Before Lao Si could answer, the overseas Chinese said angrily, "Call yourselves a defense corps? You're just a bunch of bandits! Go and fetch your commander!"

10. Thinking the overseas Chinese to be someone of importance, Lao Si hurriedly reported to Nan Ba-tian. Seeing that all the names on the greeting cards in his case were from well-known people in Canton and Hainan Island, Nan Ba-tian decided that the overseas Chinese must have influential connections. So he roared at Lao Si, "You swine! How dare you be insolent to our guest!"

11. Nan Ba-tian immediately went to the dungeon to apologize, saying, "Mr. Hong, my ignorant subordinates have offended you. Please overlook it!"

12. Nan Ba-tian planned to use the wealth and influence of the overseas Chinese to purchase some ammunition and, together with him, to wipe out the newly founded Red Army. So he tried to make amends by giving him a feast in the guest room. The bandit chief Huang Chen-shan was invited to the feast.

13. During the banquet Nan Ba-tian said, "Brother Hong, if you want to build your family fortune in your native home, you must first wipe out the Communists!" The overseas Chinese replied, "We should exert ourselves to save this fine land. But I am now returning to my native home to rebuild my ancestral temple. Let us talk the matter over after my trip."

14. Meanwhile, Lao Si, under Nan Ba-tian's orders, came that night with another thug to the water pit in the dungeon. They planned to take Qing-hua away to be sold.

15. Qing-hua climbed out of the water, then suddenly seized Lao Si's leg and threw him backwards into the water.

16. Not frightened by the whip and the fetters, the brave Qing-hua once again tried to escape from the landlord's bloody den.

17. But weakened by the wounds, Qing-hua was recaptured and dragged back by the landlord's thugs. As there was a guest present, Nan Ba-tian said impatiently with a wave of his hand, "Hurry up and sell her!"

18. The overseas Chinese saw what was happening. His quick-thinking mind thought up a plan and he said, "At the moment, my mother is living in Canton and wants to buy a maid. This. . . ." Thinking this a rare opportunity to please the guest, Nan Ba-tian consented straightaway. "By all means. She was really born lucky," he said.

19. Next morning, they left Nan's mansion. Qing-hua, following behind, watched them suspiciously.

20. Reaching Boundary Ridge the overseas Chinese dismounted, untied Qing-hau and said, "You can go home now." When she was sure he meant no harm, she replied briefly, "I don't have a home. Both my parents were killed by Nan. I want to get in touch with the Communists and join the Red Army!"

21. The overseas Chinese was overjoyed and pointed the way to Red-stone Village. After asking her name, he took out four silver coins and said, "Take this to buy something to eat on the way."

22. Qing-hua took the coins. She was deeply moved. She wanted to say something but did not know how to put it. After she had walked for a few yards she turned around and bowed—and then hurried off.

23. When they reached the forest deep in the mountains, a Red Army guard hurried over to welcome them. For, in fact, the overseas Chinese was Hong Chang-ching, Party secretary of a special unit of the Red Army, and the servant was messenger Xiao Bang. They had just been to Canton to collect the workers' contributions in support of the Red Army. Afraid of exposing the whereabouts of the divisional headquarters, they had not brought Qing-hua with them.

24. Hong Chang-ching gave his report to the divisional commander who commended them on their ingenious escape from Nan and their rescue of Qing-hua. "Tomorrow," concluded the commander, "a mass meeting will be held in Red-stone Village where the first armed revolutionary unit of women in China will be founded. The Party appoints you as its representative to this company of women fighters."

25. At night the hills were veiled in mist and rain. Hungry and worn out, Qing-hua picked her way along the mountain path. Suddenly, she spotted a cottage at the foot of the hill. "Perhaps," she thought, "I will be able to get something to eat there."

26. Creeping up to the door, Qing-hua saw a bunch of manioc roots hanging on the wall. She took one and hungrily munched it.

27. Having gulped the food, Qing-hua was collecting some raindrops to drink when she suddenly heard someone saying softly, "Hey, don't drink that! Come on in, there's water here." She gave a start and saw a figure standing in front of the doorway.

28. Following the person inside, Qing-hua discovered that it was a young man. She was a little flustered. But the young man hastily removed his turban and said, "Don't be afraid. I'm a girl too. My name's Hong-lian."

29. Puzzled, Qing-hua asked, "Elder sister, why are you dressed like a man?" "Just for self-protection," answered Hong-lian. Then Qing-hua asked her why she was all alone in the house. "My in-laws have gone to the city to worship," she answered, "and I am going to take this chance to run away and join the Red Army."

30. Qing-hua asked her whether her husband would agree. Pointing to the wooden-figure of a man on the bed, Hong-lian said bitterly, "That's my husband. He died before our wedding but I was forced by feudal customs to marry this dummy and keep it company for ten whole years!" Qing-hua said angrily, "There's really no way out for girls like us. Let's go!"

31. Next morning Qing-hua and Hong-lian hurried to Red-stone Village to find the Red Army.

32. On entering the village they saw many people going to the rally for the founding of the women's detachment. They were anxious to join when they met Hong-lian's old neighbor, A-gui, now a member of the Red Guards. Hong-lian told Qing-hua, "He ran away from the landlord's house two years ago."

33. A-gui led them to the rally. At the center stood an orderly formation of troops. Qing-hua was very eager to join their ranks. She was very excited.

34. The rally began. The divisional commander spoke briefly and forcefully, "Comrades! At present the Chiang Kai-shek reactionaries are launching frantic attacks on our Central Revolutionary Base on the mainland. The Party calls on you women who have suffered so bitterly to take up arms and open fire on the vicious reactionaries! . . ."

35. The divisional commander went on to say, "Now, on behalf of the Jiongyi Committee of the Communist Party of China and the Independent Division of the Red Army, I present the colors to China's first company of women fighters."

36. Taking hold of Hong-lian's hand, Qing-hua ran toward the rostrum. The women fighters of the Red Army were singing the march of the women's detachment as they passed in review. Catching sight of them following behind their column, a woman fighter said, "Hey, you two. Keep out of the ranks. We are having a parade!"

37. After the review, the company commander asked Qing-hua what they were doing there. She said they wanted to join the women's detachment. The company commander said, "I noticed you joined the ranks when the troops were marching past. You are very bold."

38. "Well then," said the company commander, "you two go and make out your applications, stating your reasons for wanting to join up." Qing-hua ripped open her jacket to show the marks of the whip and said, "My reason? Here's my reason!"

39. Just then the divisional commander and Hong Chang-ching walked over. Qing-hua was stunned, "How is it. . . ? The man on horseback . . . was you?" Smiling, Hong Chang-ching nodded to her and said to the divisional commander, "This is the woman I spoke about." The divisional commander said, "All right, let her stay."

40. Qing-hua and Hong-lian put on the uniform of the Red Army fighters for the first time and felt full of strength. Their new life was bringing them endless joy.

41. Qing-hua and Hong-lian underwent tough, revolutionary training and one day in spring they were ordered to reconnoiter at Coconut Village. After they had disguised themselves, they were told to be particularly careful and not to reveal their identity on any account.

42. Outside the south gate of Coconut Village, Qing-hua and Hong-lian carefully observed the position of the guns in the enemy's new fortifications.

43. At that moment, Nan Ba-tian accompanied by a bunch of his thugs, was on his way to visit his ancestral graves. The sight of him filled Qing-hua with anger and she whipped out her pistol. "What are you doing?" asked Hong-lian. "I want to take revenge!" the other replied, gritting her teeth.

44. Qing-hua fired two shots before Hong-lian could stop her.

45. Nan was hit in the left shoulder and the thugs were thrown into confusion.

46. Seeing that they had exposed their position, Hong-lian hastily dragged Qing-hua back to company headquarters. "You shouldn't have acted against the scouting rules in order to take your own revenge," the company commander said to Qing-hua sternly. "Remember you aren't the girl you were three months ago. You're a soldier now. If you keep on doing things like this you had better go your own way."

47. Seeing the company commander so angry, Qing-hua thought she was no longer wanted. With tears in her eyes, she thought, "How is it that I was wrong in firing at the landlord? The Red Army is my home, I can't leave it!"

48. When Hong Chang-ching heard about the incident he came to see Qing-hua. He hoped he might be able to help her. "Comrade Qing-hua," he said, "do you think you're the only one with wrongs to avenge? Is there any proletarian whose heart isn't soaked in tears? Can you get anywhere simply fighting alone? Don't forget you're a revolutionary fighter!"

49. Hong's words made a deep impression on Qing-hua. He wanted her to bear this lesson in mind, so he told her to go and think over her mistake. Impressed by the way Hong had dealt with the matter, the company commander criticized herself for her wrong attitude toward Qing-hua's mistake.

50. "Sister," Qing-hua said to Hong-lian, "Comrade Hong Chang-ching's way of letting comrades realize their mistakes is very good. He does it in a way you can accept from the bottom of your heart!" "Yes," Hong-lian replied, "we should learn from people like him and try to improve ourselves."

51. The next morning when the two were practicing hand-to-hand combat in their room, a comrade brought them their food. "We'll be attacking Nan Ba-tian tonight," she told them. "Really!" exclaimed Qing-hua, excitement written all over her face.

52. Without bothering about her food, she started to ask the company commander for permission to take part in the fight. Then she stopped in the doorway. "Haven't I been told to think over my mistakes?" she thought.

53. Hong-lian encouraged her, saying that nobody would remember the matter. "No," said Qing-hua firmly after a little thought. "Since I've been told to think over my mistake, I must really observe discipline." So Hong-lian said, "Then I'll go and ask the company commander on your behalf."

54. Hong Chang-ching was discussing the plan of action with other officers when Hong-lian came in to plead Qing-hua's cause. "Why didn't she come herself?" asked Hong Chang-ching. "She said she must really abide by discipline," said Hong-lian. "All right," he chuckled, "tell her to wait for orders."

55. After Hong-lian had left, Hong Chang-ching said, "Nan Ba-tian is expecting me to go back to discuss important plans with him. If I go back as a wealthy overseas Chinese merchant, I'll get him in my clutches. Then the enemy will lose their commander." All agreed to his idea.

56. Dressed once again as a wealthy overseas Chinese merchant, Hong Chang-ching arrived at Coconut Village with Qing-hua, Hong-lian, and Xiao Bang.

57. When the tyrant came out of his mansion to greet him, Hong thought, "Don't rejoice too soon. Your hour will soon come."

58. In the reception room he told Hong-lian to present Nan Ba-tian with gifts, which included rare medicinal herbs and a large amount of silver dollars. "A few native products," said Hong. "Oh, there is no need for so many gifts!" exclaimed Nan.

59. As he stood up to express his thanks, Nan suddenly uttered a groan. "Aren't you feeling well, brother?" asked Hong, pretending ignorance about what had happened. "Those Communist bandits," Nan said angrily, "took a shot at me, hitting me in the left shoulder. I must get my revenge!"

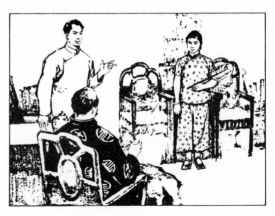

60. After a while he added, "Brother Hong, about that matter we discussed last time. . . ." Without waiting for him to finish, Hong said, "Oh, my mind's made up. I can't promise to give every thing I possess, but at least I'll do my utmost to help maintain order here on Hainan Island."

61. Nan was very pleased but the head steward remained suspicious. Alone with his master he said, "On the way to his home district and during his return journey he had to pass through Communist-held territory. How did he get through so easily? Anyway, he talks in such an arrogant way it would be impossible for him to work together with others for very long."

62. "If he were a mere nobody, I would not have troubled to make friends with him," Nan laughed. "Now go and tell Lao Si to go to the mountains and invite Huang Chenshan here to discuss some important matters." Before leaving, the head steward said, "I only hope, Commander, you'll be on your guard, otherwise it may cost you dear!"

63. After supper the head steward—a loyal lackey—stole over to Hong Chang-ching's quarters. Hong-lian and Qing-hua caught sight of him as he was eavesdropping outside the window.

64. Qing-hua promptly tipped off Hong about the spying. To make every word distinct he said in a loud voice, "Xiao Bang, you go back to Canton tomorrow and bring my mother here for a holiday. I've decided to stay here for a few more days to discuss some business with Commander Nan."

65. All was quiet in the dead of night. Hong looked at his watch and saw that it was the time for action. He told Xiao Bang to go and open the back door.

66. Xiao Bang crept over to the back door and opened it. The women fighters who had disguised themselves as village girls slipped in.

67. Qing-hua and Hong-lian tiptoed into Nan's sleeping quarters.

68. The landlord was trapped in his sleep. Giving him a contemptuous glance, Hong ordered three fires to be lit. These were the signal for the Red Army men and the women fighters to attack the defense corps that guarded the village.

69. Meanwhile, the women soldiers hidden in the village rushed into the defense corps headquarters. Gold Teeth was shot by the company commander as he drew out his pistol.

70. Coconut Village was lit up by the fires as the Red Army broke into it. Many of the defense corps members were killed, others surrendered. The village was liberated.

71. After daybreak Qing-hua marched Nan down the street. She cried out all about the crimes he had committed against two generations of her family. "Countrymen," she cried, "I was a slave in Nan Ba-tian's house. Just because my father kicked his dog, he had him beaten to death. . . ."

72. Qing-hua's story aroused the crowd who demanded that punishment be meted out to the despot who had crushed them for so many years.

73. With the parade over, Nan was kept in custody awaiting public trial. But when the cunning old man saw there was only one woman soldier guarding him, he thought of a way of escaping. He asked to go to the toilet.

74. He went into the inner room, pried up a plank in the floor and disappeared into an underground passage.

75. When the company commander came in with Qing-hua and Hong-lian to take Nan to the trial, the guard told them that he had gone to the toilet in the inner room. Qing-hua rushed in and found the uncovered hole on the floor—and Nan was nowhere to be seen.

76. She fired two shots in rapid succession into the tunnel before jumping down to chase him.

77. Nan clambered out of the other end of the tunnel and ran up the hill. At that moment, the junior steward Lao Si was on his way back with the bandit chief Huang Chen-shan. They were surprised to see Nan in such a state.

78. Nan had been so frightened by the fighting that he was unable to utter a word when the two rushed over to meet him. Looking in the direction Nan had come from, Huang Chen-shan saw a woman soldier running up the hill. He fired several shots at her. Then he and Lao Si dragged Nan off and disappeared behind the hill.

79. Qing-hua was hit and fell to the ground. In her eagerness to recapture the landlord she had been caught off guard.

80. The company commander, who had been in hot pursuit some way behind, saw Qing-hua fall and rushed up and held her in his arms.

81. Qing-hua was taken to a rear hospital for an operation on her wound. When Hong Chang-ching visited her and asked how she felt, she said, "I'm fine. A whipping from the landlord was much worse than this."

82. Several days later Hong came to see her again and was relieved to find her looking better. He told her about the rapidly developing revolutionary situation throughout the country. Overjoyed, Qing-hua was anxious to be up and about again to take part in the struggle.

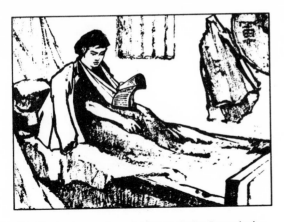

83. Qing-hua's wound was healing gradually. Remembering the Party's teachings, she read a lot during her convalescence, which helped her understand many revolutionary theories previously unknown to her.

84. Soon she was discharged from the hospital. On her way back to the unit she fell in with Hong at Boundary Ridge. She asked for permission to go along to the county town and come back with Nan Ba-tian's head. "And if you should fail?" asked Hong meaningly. "Then he'd get my head instead," was her curt reply.

85. As they walked toward Coconut Village, Hong thought about how he could make Qing-hua understand the power people possess when they fight together. Soon they were in front of Nan's mansion which now housed the local people's government.

86. In his office Hong indicated a map on the table and said, "Qing-hua, can you find Hainan Island?" She was unable to locate it. "See, it's right here," Hong pointed it out. "What a tiny place!" exclaimed Qing-hua.

87. "Coconut Village isn't even on the map, not a trace of it!" said Hong. "Now Qing-hua, think! Could a huge country like ours ever be liberated if we were to depend on the bravery of one individual alone?" Qing-hua suddenly saw the point. "You're so good at making others understand!" she laughed.

88. Impressed by Hong's knowledge, Qing-hua asked him how long he had been at school. He said that when he was small he had worked with his father on an ocean-going ship. He began school at age ten with the help of the Canton Seamen's Union which was later banned by the reactionaries. Many members were killed and his father was flung into the Pearl River. So Hong stopped going to school.

89. "Because I could speak Hainan dialect I managed to escape from Canton," said Hong. "Qing-hua, if we are to right bloody wrongs and overthrow the detestable old society, we must always depend on the collective, on the whole working class!" Each of Hong's statements struck home in Qing-hua's mind.

90. Educated by the Communist Party, Qing-hua and Hong-lian quickly raised their class consciousness. They were eager to join the Party. In their letters of application for membership they wrote, "I will carry the struggle through to the end for the complete emancipation of the whole working class and for the realization of Communism!"

91. One year later Chiang Kai-shek sent his Central Guards Brigade to Hainan to wipe out the Jiongyi Independent Division. Since his escape Nan Ba-tian had gone about quietly in the county town, hoping for a come-back. Hearing about the arrival of the brigade, he and members of the local gentry went to the wharf to welcome the troops.

92. Over the dinner table Nan proposed to Brigade Commander Chen, "Our troops should make use of Hainan's special features in waging war. Concentrate our forces at one point and launch surprise attacks. In this way the enemy will be unable to evacuate all the civilians and property from their new area, even if they do find out about the movement of the government forces."

93. "Our unit has come to Hainan from Kiangsi, firmly resolved that the Communists on this island must be completely wiped out," the brigade commander nodded. "Full consideration must be given to Mr. Nan's suggestion. I'll instantly order my three infantry regiments to set out tonight on two routes—left and right!"

94. Having heard of the enemy's plan, Hong and the company commander started to organize the withdrawal of the women's detachment, the Red Guards, the government functionaries and their families. In the meantime, Xiao Bang galloped up and handed Hong a dispatch from division headquarters.

95. After reading the dispatch Hong said, "Company Commander, you take the first and second platoons and join the main forces to thrust into the enemy rear. The third platoon and the comrades of company headquarters will come with me to Boundary Ridge to pin down the enemy." The company commander wanted to intercept the enemy, but Hong would not hear of it. Reluctantly she said good-by to him.

96. Hong-lian was looking after her comrades wounded in the fighting, when Qing-hua ran up to tell her to withdraw them immediately.

97. After the wounded were evacuated from the village, Hong Chang-ching led the last group of women fighters to Boundary Ridge.

98. At dawn the Kuomintang troops occupied Coconut Village. Then under cover of artillery fire they started to attack Boundary Ridge. Entrenched on the hilltop the women soldiers of the third platoon put up a stubborn resistance, beating off several enemy attacks.

99. Their attacks having failed, Nan Ba-tian told Huang Chen-shan to lead his thugs in a charge. Before he went, Nan offered him three bowls of wine.

100. Huang swallowed a paper charm to "protect" himself from bullets and tore up the hill at the head of his men. They were wielding broad-bladed swords.

101. The women soldiers had run short of ammunition. "Qing-hua," said Hong, "we've fulfilled our task of interception. You lead the first and second squads and the wounded and pull back at once, while the third squad and I will cover your withdrawal." Qing-hua, however, insisted on staying at the front.

102. Hong fixed his eyes on the girl, then in an outburst of feeling said, "Comrade Qing-hua, the Party has approved your application and Hong-lian's for admission to the Party. From now on you're a vanguard fighter of the proletariat. If we should fail to get away, then you Party members who have pulled back will be the mainstay in the future. You will shoulder the responsibility till victory is ours!"

103. Noticing her hesitancy Hong said earnestly, "Go on, accept your first assignment as a member of the Party." Qing-hua looked at him with emotion, then took from her pocket the four silver coins that he had given her. "Comrade Chang-ching," she said, "here are my first Party dues."

104. Hong watched till Qing-hua and the others were out of sight. Then he turned and saw Huang Chen-shan and his men charging and brandishing their swords. He trained his machine gun on Huang who was running in front of his men.

105. The bandit chief was shot dead before he reached Hong's position. Hong himself was seriously wounded.

106. Shortly after the women fighters had withdrawn to the other side of the hill, the scout reported that there was no news from the front. "Check up on the weapons," said Qing-hua firmly, "and gather all the ammunition together while I go back to see how things are."

107. In a dark ancestral temple Nan was complaining to Battalion Commander Hu. "Sir," he said, "we've lost a whole company just fighting a small detachment of women!" "Where are the main Communist forces?" demanded Hu furiously. "Just get me out of the clutches of these women!"

108. An orderly came in and handed a dispatch to Hu. After reading it he said, "We've been split up by the Communists. We'll proceed to brigade headquarters at daybreak tomorrow. So we'll be getting out of this inferno of a place!"

109. The battalion commander left in an angry mood. Presently Lao Si came in to announce, "Commander, he's come to again." Seriously wounded, Hong Chang-ching had lost consciousness and was captured by the enemy. But despite their torture he had not given the enemy any information.

110. When Hong was brought in, Nan pointed to a sheet of paper on the table, which bore the heading "My Confession." "Mr. Hong," he said, "if you will call on the women's detachment to surrender, you can still have riches and honor." Hong held his head high and looked proudly at the landlord.

111. With a sarcastic laugh Hong took the brush and crossed out the words "My Confession." Then he wrote:

Chop off my head if you wish,
My cause is just!
Others will follow behind
When I am under the sod!

112. "Just fine!" Nan roared in a fury. "Now you can die for your just cause! Drag him out!"

113. Hong was tied to a huge tree. Behind him were bundles of cotton which had been soaked in kerosene. He looked for the last time at the lovely countryside. Fixing his fierce eyes on the murderers, he shouted at the top of his voice, "Down with the Kuomintang! Long live the Communist Party!"

114. Within seconds Hong was enveloped in flames and died a hero's death. Qing-hua saw all that was happening from the hilltop, but she could do nothing. If she did, the whole campaign might be adversely affected. She was overcome with grief as she watched, unable to save her close comrade-in-arms from the enemy.

115. With tears in her eyes Qing-hua retraced her steps.

116. On the hill slope she found Hong Chang-ching's brief case. It contained the four silver coins and the two applications for Party membership written by Hong-lian and herself. Memories flooded back to her as she solemnly vowed, "I'll carry on the work left unfinished by Comrade Hong Chang-ching, unite with my comrades, and carry the struggle through to the end!"

117. When Qing-hua returned, her comrades sensed something was wrong. Controlling herself Qing-hua said, "The comrades at the front have all died the death of heroes. Comrade Chang-ching has given his life for our glorious cause!"

118. Every heart was ablaze with hatred. "Comrades," said Qing-hua, "the Party organization still exists. We must shoulder the tasks left unfulfilled by the martyrs and fight to the bitter end!"

119. Xiao Bang arrived at noon with an order from the division commander. "The enemy troops have been routed by our main forces," he told the women fighters. "As Nan Ba-tian may attempt to escape, the division commander orders you to do your best to pin him down. You are to hold out till the main forces arrive at six o'clock tomorrow evening!"

120. The scout sent out to reconnoiter also returned to report that Nan Ba-tian was getting ready to escape and that he had arrested many villagers in preparation for a massacre. Qing-hua called the Party members to a meeting where her plan of operation was approved.

121. At noon the next day Qing-hua and the other women fighters, dressed as villagers, went to Coconut Village.

122. Nan's mansion was in a commotion as the stewards packed up things and moved cases. The landlord was also busy, frantically destroying his furniture and ornaments so that nothing of value would be left behind.

123. Lao Si came into the reception room. "Commander," he said, "we've rounded up all the paupers in the village. Will you have a look?"

124. Nan came to the square in front of his house. "Well, paupers, you didn't expect this, did you?" he shouted. "I'm going to make sure you don't dig up my ancestral tombs after I leave! But if any of you shouts 'Down with the Communist Party!' I spare his life!"

125. The villagers did not say a word. They glared sullenly at him. "What, none of you will shout it?" he threatened. Suddenly an old man raised his hand and cried, "Down with the despots and evil gentry!"

126. In a rage the landlord ordered the old man to be killed. At this point Qing-hua and her comrades, who had caught the enemy unaware and quickly occupied Nan's mansion, appeared on the scene.

127. The members of the defense corps were dumfounded by the sudden appearance of the women soldiers. Nan Ba-tian was captured.

128. The landlord was led into the reception room in his mansion. "I tell you, the Red Army has routed the Kuomintang troops and is now coming to this country," Qing-hua shouted angrily. "Tell your men to surrender at once!" Pretending to be calm Nan said, "Allow me to take my own life."

129. Qing-hua threw him a dagger. Nan reached for it with a trembling hand, but immediately drew back. With a scornful smile Qing-hua said, "At the first glance I saw you had the heart of a wolf but the courage of a rabbit!"

130. "There need be no hatred between us," pleaded the landlord. "Let bygones be bygones. Leave me some way out. I'll evacuate my men and leave all my property to you. I promise to leave the army and never come back here again." "A fine idea! You'll just come back and attack us," retorted Qing-hua.

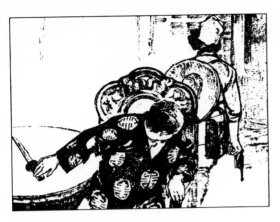

131. There were cheers outside—the main Red Army forces had joined up with the women's detachment. When Qing-hua turned to look out the window, Nan Ba-tian, grinding his teeth, reached for the dagger.

132. Before he could pick up the dagger, Qing-hua had fired twice and the tyrant dropped full length on the floor.

133. Amid thunderous cheers Qing-hua reported briefly to the company commander about the battle they had fought. The commander and the other comrades praised her for having fulfilled her assignments.

134. The women's detachment had withstood hard times and performed outstanding exploits. Soon after the battle a second company of the detachment was organized with Qing-hua as its Party representative.

135. Standing before the ranks of the new fighters, Qing-hua said with emotion, "From today on, the hundred and twenty of you will be glorious fighters. . . . We must carry forward the splendid tradition of the first company of the women's detachment! We must learn from the martyrs who have given their lives! We shall advance and defeat all the Nan Ba-tians."

136. At dawn the heroic women's detachment was on the march again. The Revolution was surging forward and they were marching to wipe out all the Kuomintang reactionaries.

碧海丹心

BRAVERY ON THE DEEP BLUE SEAS

Size 12.5 x 10 cm

Original story by Liang Xin

Adapted by Wan Jia-chun

Illustrated by Xu Jin

Published by the Shanghai People's Art
*   Publishing Co., Shanghai, 1965*

Number of copies printed: 200,000

1. In 1949, after our great liberating armies had liberated the mainland as fast as a firecracker, the Chiang dynasty was smashed to smithereens. In the far south a small bunch of the Chiang bandit army attempted to escape from the Leichou peninsula and secure Hainan Island in order to make a desperate fight to the finish there.

2. Just as the last of the Chiang bandit army's infantry and equipment had been embarked, ready to leave for the island, the advance guard of our Army charged onto the beach.

3. Ai Dehua, captain of the enemy warship Taihua saw our Army burst down onto the beaches, about to capture the small boats becalmed there. He smiled coldly and said, "I'll use my guns to teach the Red Army the difference between a warship and a fishing boat!"

4. The enemy shells rained down among the several hundred fishing boats and destroyed them. Then as our artillery began pounding them, the enemy retreated in confusion toward Hainan Island.

5. Our Army was quartered in a fishing village beside the sea. On returning from the camp meeting, the commander of the No. 1 "Steel" Company, Xiao Ding, saw an old fisherman standing by the house selected as company headquarters and asked him if there were any boats nearby. To his surprise the old man walked off without saying a word.

6. Somewhat surprised, Xiao Ding entered the company headquarters and saw an eighteen- or nineteen-year-old girl standing behind the door. The communications aide Xiao Hong told him that apart from the girl, only the old man whom he had just met outside the door lived there.

7. Xiao Ding looked around inside and saw that there were two rooms and that the main one had been taken over by the company while the old fisherman and his daughter had been squeezed into the side room. Xiao Ding was annoyed and criticized Xiao Hong.

8. Xiao Ding had Xiao Hong move the company command post into the side room to leave the main room free for the old man and his daughter. He noticed that the girl was standing to one side listening, so he stopped talking and helped Xiao Hong to move the things through.

9. That evening the old fisherman returned. As soon as he came into the room he noticed that the command post had been moved into the side room and he was very surprised. His daughter said to him in a whisper, "This powerful Army practices what it preaches; for example, as soon as he came in, the company commander ordered his aide to move the command post into the side room . . ."

10. The old man's name was Jin Da-yi. His wife had died a long time previously and he passed his days catching fish with his daughter, Jin Xiao-mei. He listened to what she said but made no reply as he poured himself a bowl of wine. He was just about to drink it, not expecting Xiao Ding to walk in at that moment.

11. Xiao Ding came and sat beside the table and was about to strike up a conversation when to his surprise the old man said, "You've come to ask for a boat again, haven't you?" Xiao Ding, pleased, replied, "Old man, you've certainly guessed right!"

12. Jin Da-yi drank a bowl of wine and then asked, "Have your people got warships and airplanes?" And then, looking straight at Xiao Ding, he said, his voice full of emotion, "The channel between here and Hainan is filled with the bones of the laboring people, for many during the last sixty years have died under the guns of foreign warships. . . ."

13. Xiao Ding said, "Little boats can get broken up, men can become seasick, and there are all sorts of other things that can go wrong . . . but nevertheless we still intend to liberate Hainan using the little boats!" The old man did not believe that Hainan could be liberated with small boats nor could he convince Xiao Ding, so he replied, "I'm not too clear about the boats in the village!"

14. Xiao Ding looked at the old man with disappointment, glanced at Xiao-mei, and then took his leave. As soon as he stepped outside the door he heard the two starting to argue.

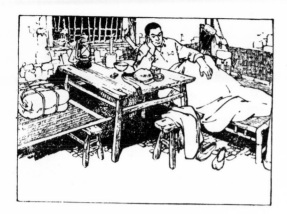

15. Xiao Ding went into the company HQ, switched off the light, and lay down on the small bamboo frame bed but, deeply worried, was unable to fall asleep.

16. He left the company HQ and went down to take a walk by the coast. As he was walking by a field of cut cane, his foot struck something. Pulling aside some palm leaves to see what he was treading on, he discovered a hidden boat!

17. Looking around, he found four more boats besides this one. He carefully covered up the boats as he had found them. On the way back to the company HQ he felt elated and began quietly to sing a favorite song.

18. Coming into the command HQ he saw Su Cheng, the political instructor, who had just come back from making arrangements for boats. Xiao Ding controlled his excitement and held back the good news of his discovery while Su Cheng told him of his attempts to find some.

19. When Su Cheng had finished eating, Xiao Ding, in high spirits, told him, "Old Su, just now I discovered five boats but I don't know who the owners are." Instructor Su delightedly replied, "As long as we've found the boats, it should not be too difficult to find their owners."

20. Early the next morning Xiao Ding and Su Cheng went to look at the boats and Su Cheng immediately ordered the second and third platoon leaders and several soldiers from fishing families to get out the boats. He also ordered the leader of the third platoon to start beating a gong to bring the owners to take command of their boats.

21. When the villagers heard the gong, their curiosity was aroused and they tried to see what was going on from a distance. Su Cheng said that since the area had only just been liberated, the masses had not had time to get to know our Army and therefore they would have to do some mass work. They all sat down to discuss it. One of the soldiers said, "We need the boats, no one has come forward to claim them, why don't we use them?"

22. While they were discussing this, a middle-aged Army man, his hair streaked with gray, appeared from the direction of the dunes. It was Commander Ding of forward headquarters. He had come to discuss plans with Xiao Ding and Su Cheng. Seeing that the comrades were discussing problems, he stood to one side.

23. As soon as Su Cheng looked up and saw Commander Ding standing by the boats, he stood up and called a greeting. Commander Ding said, "The boats belong to the masses and must be returned to them. Your opinion was perfectly correct—you must do more mass work."

24. Next, Commander Ding approached the soldier who had wanted to take the boats and, as they strolled along, said to him, "At the time, why did you want to join the Liberation Army?" The soldier replied that the Liberation Army was good and the commander asked, "Good in what way?" and he replied with a smile, "Because the Liberation Army is fighting for us laboring people."

25. The commander said, "What if at the very beginning we had moved off with your family's plot of land and old hut?" The soldier replied, "Our old hut and strip of land could not be moved." The commander's tone grew more serious. "But these boats can be moved, so you would just take them?" The soldier suddenly saw what the commander was getting at and he realized the error in his thinking.

26. From that time, Xiao Ding and Su Cheng both encouraged the soldiers to do mass work and to repair the boats. After a few days the five boats were looking as good as new. Xiao Ding called the masses of the village together for a meeting and asked the owners of the boats to come and take command of them.

27. The fishermen were still a bit suspicious and no one moved. Just at that moment two enemy planes came flying toward them. The soldiers quickly pushed the boats into the water, preparing to hide each one separately. Jin Xiao-mei suddenly dashed to one of the boats and took the rudder.

28. The enemy planes circled low over the boats and then after a burst of gunfire flew off. Xiao Ding asked Xiao-mei, "Miss, who do the boats belong to after all?" Xiao-mei replied naughtily, "The boat belongs to the family of the helmsman." And at that Xiao Ding suddenly realized whose they were.

29. Xiao-mei suddenly shouted, "Blood!" Xiao Ding felt with his hand and discovered blood on his head and, as if nothing much was the matter, replied, "It's nothing much, just a surface scratch!" Xiao-mei took off her scarf to bandage up the wound but Xiao Ding stopped her.

30. On returning to the company HQ, Xiao Ding excitedly told Su Cheng that the owner of the boats had now been found.

31. Su Cheng asked him what the next step should be and Xiao Ding replied, "We must be determined. Tonight we will help the masses go out fishing and at the same time learn how to sail the boats." Su Cheng was impressed by his resolve and agreed that they should put to sea on a fishing trip.

32. While they were speaking, the No. 2 Squad leader came in and Xiao Ding happily called out, "You've come at just the right moment! Second Squad leader, aren't you from a fisherman's family in the Pohai Gulf? Do you think you can still manage your old trade?" The No. 2 Squad leader replied, "Setting the sails and following the fish? Yes, I can do it!"

Couldn't be better. Start your preparations right away!

33. Xiao Ding told him that he intended to gather together all those in the company who had had experience in handling a boat and that they would go out that evening. Delighted, the No. 2 Squad leader replied, "We're going to arm and protect the fishing boats! Excellent! Please give that task of organizing the group to me!" Xiao Ding granted his request.

34. That afternoon the No. 2 Squad leader mobilized each ship captain in turn. When they heard that the boats were to be armed and protected they were delighted and at once set about erecting the masts, hoisting the sails, cleaning the nets, and getting everything ready to put to sea.

35. That evening all the soldiers of the company went down to the beach to see off Xiao Ding, the No. 2 Squad leader, and seven or eight other soldiers. When Xiao Ding and the others were aboard, the five boats weighed anchor. Their fishing lights shining, the little boats sailed out to sea.

36. Xiao Ding and the No. 2 Squad leader were on the Jin family's boat. The old man, Jin Da-yi, stood at the bow like a commander while his daughter Xiao-mei skillfully took the helm. Xiao Ding thought that where the old man stood he would put his rifles and tommy guns. . . .

37. When the No. 2 Squad leader asked Xiao Ding if he felt seasick he replied, "I simply don't believe in seasickness, class consciousness can overcome anything!" The No. 2 Squad leader shook his head and said with a smile, "They're two different things. Ha! Ha!"

38. The No. 2 Squad leader took out some salted vegetable and stuffed it into Xiao Ding's hand, saying, "Take it and when you are sick, chew a bit." Xiao Ding began to refuse, but the No. 2 Squad leader repeatedly urged him to accept and so finally Xiao Ding put it into his pocket. By this time the boat was already right out to sea and they began to spread the nets.

39. Xiao Ding, however, was unable to keep his balance in the heaving little boat and he fell over. Jin Da-yi and the No. 2 Squad leader rushed to help him but Xiao Ding pushed them aside saying, "Grandpa, don't worry about me. I came along with you to find out what it was like. Go back to the fishing!"

40. They brought in catch after catch of fish until the hold was piled high with their twisting and jumping silvery bodies. Xiao Ding now felt really sick and in between pulling in the nets he vomited over the side. He thought of eating some salted vegetable but no sooner had he put it to his mouth than his hand fell to his side, exhausted.

41. Jin Da-yi held him up and poured him some water, telling him to drink, then bring it up. At the same time he shouted to Xiao-mei, "We've got enough fish now; let's hoist sail and go home!"

42. The sail was hoisted and the little boat began racing before the wind. The No. 2 Squad leader stood holding his tommy gun, keeping a lookout ahead. They had not gone far when he saw the white beam of a searchlight.

43. Shouting "Danger ahead!" he ordered the fishing lights extingushed and then reported to Xiao Ding, "Company Commander, there's a light ahead! Looks like the enemy!" Xiao Ding jumped up, drew his revolver, and said, "Where?" The No. 2 Squad leader pointed out the searchlight beam.

44. After a moment another beam appeared and the two beams crisscrossed back and forth across the sea. It looked as if the enemy had seen the fishing lights. Xiao Ding ordered the No. 2 Squad leader to lower the sail and cut off the mast.

45. And now they could clearly see a Chiang bandit warship searching its way toward them. The fishing boat, however, had no means of moving and was being washed by the waves slowly toward the warship. The No. 2 Squad leader prepared to jump into the sea and swim to the mast in order to set it afire and draw off the enemy.

46. Xiao Ding stopped him and then told Jin Da-yi to hold on to the rudder. Jin Da-yi said, "What's the point? I'll hold you up in the sea; as long as I'm alive I can look after you, Company Leader Xiao!" Xiao Ding grasped his hand firmly but said no.

47. While they had been talking, the two boats had been drawing closer and they could now clearly make out the gun turrets, bridge, and even the muzzles of the guns on the warship. Xiao Ding decided to defeat the enemy with cunning.

48. Xiao Ding commanded Jin Da-yi and Xiao-mei to get down in the boat and the No. 2 Squad leader to take the tiller. Slowly the little boat drew closer to the warship and to the blind spot beneath the beam of the searchlight.

49. When the fishing boat was about 100 meters away from the warship, it was completely engulfed in its bow wave. Jin Da-yi gave Xiao Ding a piece of driftwood to hang onto in case they were capsized. Xiao Ding didn't say a word but shook Jin Da-yi's hand again and again.

50. Xiao Ding shouted out, "Keep her ahead!" and the No. 2 Squad leader gritted his teeth and threw his weight on the tiller to bring the boat to starboard. As if jumping with surprise, the fishing boat was borne toward the enemy warship.

51. The warship grazed past the fishing boat and was unable to see them. Xiao Ding let out a long sigh, "Phew, that was lucky. But I wonder what will happen to the other boats?" Jin Da-yi watched the direction in which the enemy ship was going and said, "Don't worry, it's leaving the bay and returning to Hainan."

52. The fishing boats safely returned to Cape Jinsha, where the Army was quartered. Su Cheng, Xiao Hong, and a crowd of soldiers lifted Xiao Ding off the boat onto a stretcher. Shaking Su Cheng's hand, Xiao Ding said: "We bumped into the enemy! It was a pity we had no larger guns at hand or we would have socked them one!"

53. Xiao Ding asked if the other boats had returned and Su Cheng told him that they had all long since gotten back. Su Cheng took off his own padded jacket and covered Xiao Ding with it, saying, "Since you were so sick, you should rest up for the next few days!"

54. After a few steps, Xiao Ding asked who was duty officer. The No. 2 Squad leader said he was. Xiao Ding then instructed him to level the sandy area to the west of the village and then rig up some temporary swinging drawbridge-like structures, ready for some dry-land practice.

55. Two days later the practice ground was completed. Company HQ invited some of the young fishermen to act as instructors and they began to practice walking on a heavy deck, swimming, and tying knots. Xiao Ding couldn't bring himself to stay in bed and went around to each platoon to find out how their practice was coming along.

56. That evening, when the soldiers were returning to the village after their day's practice, they suddenly saw Jin Da-yi and another old man named Er Gong carrying a tray and an announcement written on red paper. They were accompanied by the whole village, young and old, and were standing waiting by the village gate.

57. Su Cheng went ahead and asked Jin Da-yi if there was some matter to discuss. Jin Da-yi gravely replied that there was and requested the comrades to face them. The soldiers then formed up abreast opposite the villagers. Er Gong held up the document and began to read it.

58. When Er Gong had finished reading, Xiao Ding raised his fist and shouted, "Thanks for the people's support!" Then Jin Da-yi took three bowls of wine from the tray and gave one each to Su Cheng and Xiao Ding and kept one for himself. They raised the bowls and drained them in a single gulp.

59. Several days later the forward command, hearing of what had been going on, requested Xiao Ding to send a comrade to report. Xiao Ding was very embarrassed and said to Su Cheng, "Headquarters wants to make us a model for the whole army, but what have we done! What are we going to say?"

60. Xiao Ding asked Su Cheng to go to the forward command to report and at the same time to discuss their future plans with Commander Ding. He reckoned that the whole company needed to practice on dry land for another four or five days before going out to sea for a trial.

61. On the fifth day Commander Ding came back with Su Cheng. Xiao Ding introduced the commander to Jin Da-yi and the commander looked into the plans for the trial sea exercises with them. After checking their preparations, he finally agreed that they should put to sea that evening.

62. The soldiers and fishermen started getting ready. By evening the beach was a scene of bustling activity and the soldiers' fighting spirit was high.

63. Commander Ding had a word with Xiao Ding about the meaning of the upcoming exercise. He said that it was the key to the success or failure of the entire Hainan campaign. Xiao Ding was nonplused when he heard this.

64. The commander instructed him, saying, "You are the first company in the entire Army to put to sea. If you make contact with the enemy, we shall learn from your experience the answer to the important question of whether or not fishing boats can stand up to warships." Xiao Ding replied firmly, "I'm convinced they can!"

65. Commander Ding went with Xiao Ding down to the beach and Xiao Ding climbed aboard. The commander's final instructions were, "If in fact you do make contact with the enemy, make sure to keep close to the wind and only open fire within one hundred meters. Keep a cool head and remain firm in the sight of death!"

66. At 7 p.m. the six single-masted boats sailed out with the breeze. The No. 2 Platoon leader was on Boat 2 which took the lead, while Xiao Ding was on Boat 1 along with the No. 2 Squad leader, Xiao Hong, the machine-gunner Old Chen, and two soldiers on the 60-millimeter cannon. Xiao-mei was at the tiller.

67. When the boats were out in the open sea, an enemy night-reconnaissance plane appeared and began circling above them. The navigation lights on the six boats were immediately extinguished.

68. A wind rose and the flotilla surged through the waves. At this moment a loud-speaker message came from Su Cheng's boat and Xiao Hong reported to Xiao Ding, "The political instructor says . . . they are seasick . . . they are all seasick."

69. Xiao Ding knew that they were now near the middle of the straits separating Hainan from the mainland, and since most of the men were lying down, it was obvious that they must have been pretty sick. So he told Xiao Hong to signal Su Cheng on the loud-speaker, asking if they should continue with the planned deep-sea exercises.

70. The political instructor replied, "If we return to the area covered by our Army's guns from the coast, we shall avoid any trouble." Xiao Ding agreed and he ordered Xiao Hong to signal the other boats to turn around immediately and form up as before behind Boats 2 and 3.

71. When Boat 3 under the No. 3 Platoon leader received the signal, it quickly sailed over to Xiao Ding's boat, came alongside, and lowered the sail. Xiao Ding asked what had happened to Boat 2 and the answer was "We cannot get through to them."

72. Xiao Ding immediately ordered Boat 3 to return with the other boats toward the mainland and then went over to Xiao-mei and said, "Xiao-mei, we've got a tough job: we've got to go and find Boat 2." Xiao-mei nodded.

73. At this moment the Chiang bandit gang's warship "Taihua" and two gunboats, the "Wuwei" and the "Wu-yuan," appeared, coming down the center of the strait. As soon as they had received the report from the recon-naissance plane, they had dashed out to start a sweep for our Army's fishing boats.

74. Boat 2 was heaving in heavy seas. No. 2 Platoon leader blew his bugle with all his might but heard no reply. The helmsman, Er Gong, said to him, "They've prob-ably all returned home. Let's also go back." The No. 2 Platoon leader shook his head. "Without the order we cannot set back. Let's look for them toward the left!"

75. Just as No. 2 Platoon was searching for Xiao Ding, Xiao Ding was looking for them. As dawn appeared in the east, Xiao Ding heard the boom of the enemy warships' guns. He glanced through his binoculars and said to Xiao-mei, "Let out the sail, Xiao-mei, let out the sail!" The little boat, its sails fully hoisted, ran before the wind in the direction from which the gunfire was coming.

76. The boat upon which the enemy was firing was none other than Boat 2 which Xiao Ding had been searching for. It had just been hit and could not move. As soon as the No. 2 Platoon leader saw Xiao Ding coming toward them at full speed, he shouted, "Company leader!" and his eyes filled with tears.

77. In order to protect the No. 2 Platoon leader's men, Xiao Ding ordered the No. 2 Squad leader to ready the mortar. The No. 2 Squad leader gauged the distance; the enemy warship was about 1,500 meters away, out of range of the mortar. With a wave of his fist, Xiao Ding ordered him to "fire anyway, in order to tempt the enemy in!"

78. Shot after shot was fired toward the enemy, each one falling short in the sea. The captain of the "Taihua," Ai Dehua, smiled scornfully and said, "This is a farce." He ordered his second-in-command to open fire on Xiao Ding's boat.

79. The enemy's main guns fired simultaneously. After firing a few shots, Ai Dehua ordered them to stop and said to the second-in-command, "Prepare to capture the enemy boats!"

80. When the "Taihua" was about 200 meters away from Xiao Ding's boat, it slowed down almost to a stop and began gliding closer: 100 meters, 50 meters . . . a shout came down from its deck, "Brothers of the Commie Army, stand by to secure a hawser, stand by. . . ."

81. The "Taihua" began to draw up alongside the fishing boat. Xiao Ding's eyes were fixed on her and the blood was pounding in his veins. He could hear the commander's instruction: "Keep a cool head and remain firm in the sight of death!"

82. The hawser was thrown down from the enemy warship, but since no one took it, it was slowly hauled back. A voice kept on calling to them to surrender and to catch the hawser; if they did not they would be pulverized.

83. Yet again the hawser came hissing down toward the boat, but this time Xiao Ding furiously raised his head, stretched out his hand, and grabbed hold of it. The men on the boat were speechless with surprise when they saw their company leader do this.

84. Using all his strength Xiao Ding pulled on the hawser and said in a whisper, "Hand grenades!" No. 2 Squad leader understood and immediately eased out a grenade from his belt. The other soldiers followed suit.

85. Quick as lightning Xiao Ding wound the hawser round the mast and shouted, "Tweak their tail! Fire!" A hand grenade soared up onto the after deck of the warship and a whole bunch of the enemy sailors fell to the deck.

86. The hand grenades fell as thick as rain on the warship's deck and many of the enemy were killed or wounded. Ai Dehua screamed in a tremendous panic, "Start the engines! Start the engines! Cut the hawser! . . ."

87. The hawser was cut and the enemy ship raced off in a panic. Watching it disappear into the distance, Xiao Ding said, "Ha! I thought we were going to capture her but after wasting half the day we've only managed to salvage a bit of steel hawser!"

88. When the enemy had escaped to 1,000 meters distance, they began to open fire on Xiao Ding's boat, and in the course of this barrage the boat was hit. One of the soldiers manning the mortar was killed and Xiao Ding was wounded in the waist. The No. 2 Squad leader and Xiao-mei quickly swam over to help him.

89. Fortunately, Political Instructor Su's boat arrived and they towed the damaged boat into the safety of the coastal waters within protective range of our Army's guns. The "Taihua" fired off several rounds after them, giving the heroic Boat 1 a sendoff....

90. As they drew close to Cape Jinsha, they could see that the beach was crowded with soldiers and fishermen who threw their caps in the air to welcome back the fishing boats. Xiao Ding and Su Cheng thought it odd that there were so many people on the beach.

91. When Xiao Ding heard the slogans being shouted on the beach—"Welcome back 'Steel Company,' welcome to the heroes in the fishing boats who beat an enemy warship"—he felt very uneasy and said, "Welcome us? That's too much, we haven't captured the enemy ship yet!"

92. Su Cheng helped Xiao Ding sit down beside the mast and thoughtfully inquired after his wound. Xiao Ding said, "It's nothing, it doesn't show. When we disembark, give me a hand and we'll say I just strained my back!"

93. Xiao Ding disembarked and reported to the commander the circumstances in which his boat had been destroyed by the enemy. Ever since the squadron had put to sea, Commander Ding had stood on the coast the whole night. Now when he saw them safely back, he felt extremely happy.

94. Commander Ding listened until Xiao Ding had finished and then let out a burst of laughter. "I never said anything about bringing back glittering war trophies, but in all history you are the first to send a 1,500-ton armored warship scuttling off using only a fishing boat!"

95. As Commander Ding was speaking, Xiao Ding fainted into Su Cheng's arms. The soldiers quickly carried him to a jeep; Commander Ding took off his greatcoat and carefully covered Xiao Ding with it.

96. As the jeep was about to move off, Xiao Ding regained consciousness and, seeing the political instructor beside him, quietly enjoined him, "Take . . . take Hainan Island, but don't leave me out!" Su Cheng nodded: "Take it easy and get well!"

97. Meanwhile the captain of the "Taihua," Ai Dehua, following his defeat by Boat 1 and his hasty withdrawal, returned to headquarters to report. He said to his commander, a senior general, that this time once again they had won "a glorious victory."

98. The bandit general was furious and fixing Ai Dehua with a stare, he said, "Lies! For a navy man to falsely report a battle action is shameless, shameless!" Ai Dehua deliberately pretended to be affronted, "Commander-in-chief, you cannot treat a navy captain like this."

99. "Navy? I am commander-in-chief of the army, navy, and airforce of Hainan at a time of emergency!" The bandit general walked back and forth saying, "Painful! Painful! The party and the army used good money to train you, they sent you to England, they sent you to America. . . ."

100. At this juncture an assistant brought in a telegram saying, "The navy department is in accord with the commander-in-chief's suggestion with regard to Captain Ai Dehua. . . ." As soon as he heard this, Ai Dehua's face turned pale and his eyes filled with tears.

101. "Get out," barked the commander-in-chief, but Ai Dehua continued, "Commander-in-chief! I implore you, don't kill me in front of the crew and the sailors." The commander-in-chief paid no attention to his pitiful entreaties.

102. The commander-in-chief let out a snort and strode out of the building. Ai Dehua followed at his heels.

103. The bandit general reviewed the sailors at the harbor and then announced, "Captain Ai Dehua, formerly of the "Taihua," has been promoted to rear admiral of the defense fleet." This unexpected decision both surprised and delighted Ai Dehua and for a moment he was quite speechless. . . .

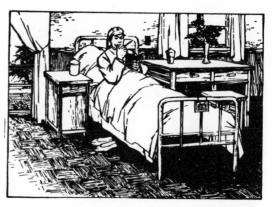

104. It was now the spring of 1950 and three months had passed since Xiao Ding had been wounded and entered the hospital. During these three months he hadn't been lying idle but had spent all his time thinking and reading about the tactics of how small boats could defeat warships.

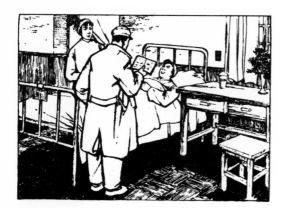

105. On this particular day Commander Ding had come to visit Xiao Ding who, overtired, had fallen fast asleep. The commander saw a small notebook by the bedside, on the cover of which was written, "The equipment, organization, and tactics of armed escort vessels."

106. Standing beside the bed, the commander read through Xiao Ding's little notebook and then with deep emotion stroked his forehead. He tore out the last leaf of the notebook, wrote something on it, and then left, taking the notebook with him.

107. When Xiao Ding awoke and read the note left by Commander Ding, he felt very excited. He opened the window and saw trucks, guns, and cars all going toward the front.

108. Xiao Ding longed to get back to the front. Following his determined requests, the rear hospital agreed to his return.

109. When he got back to the company, Xiao Ding threw himself into sea exercises along with the soldiers and also experimented with organizing armed escort boats.

110. One evening before the sea battle for Hainan, Xaio Ding received orders to go to the forward headquarters. Commander Ding informed him that headquarters had checked out several of his ideas about the use of armed fishing boats and had decided that they could be utilized. As he spoke he led Xiao Ding to a relief model.

111. On the model of the straits between the mainland and Hainan were placed five fishing boats surrounding a warship. The commander asked Xiao Ding, "To have five of the fishing boats surround one warship is sound enough, but what if five warships surround one fishing boat? What will you do then?"

112. Xiao Ding was at a loss for an answer for he had simply not thought of such a problem. The commander reminded him, "Go for the rudder and go for the leading vessel!" Understanding, Xiao Ding said, "Right! Seize the enemy flagship and attack it with all one's forces!" He then requested the commander to place him in charge of the armed escort boats.

113. The commander said, "It's no easy matter for fishing boats to take on a ship like the "Taihua." It has a large displacement and high speeds." Xiao Ding resolutely replied, "No, it's not easy. But given the opportunity, I'll do my utmost to seize it." The commander patted him on the shoulder and granted Xiao Ding's request to take command of the armed escort.

114. On the evening of the next day the preparations for putting to sea were all completed. Several hundred boats were drawn up in neat rows. Jin Da-yi and his daughter this time stood on the command ship, for they had been granted the honor of being selected as helmsmen of the command ship.

115. Before setting out to cross the straits and do battle, the tens of thousands of soldiers held a final meeting. Commander Ding stood under the ceremonial embarkation point for the command ship and, together with the soldiers, vowed, "In order to unite the sacred territory of our fatherland, we will resolutely defeat the warships and win back command of the seas and raise the five-starred red flag on Hainan Island!"

116. Next could be heard the sound of firecrackers, gongs, and drums and the soldiers' singing. The crowds on the beaches cheered and shouted happily and waved red flags to send them off.

117. Three red signal rockets soared into the sky and the fleet hoisted their sails; the several hundred boats filled with heroic sons and daughters of the fatherland began to sail toward the center channel of the straits.

118. Xiao Ding's Boat 1 was positioned at the head on the command ship's port bow. Everybody on board stood at battle stations, staring into the distance ahead. When it was completely dark, three red lights suddenly appeared on the southern horizon.

119. "It's the Black Strumpet!" Signalman Xiao Hong reported the sighting of an enemy plane to Xiao Ding. Xiao Ding ordered, "Prepare to knock her out!"

120. Xiao Ding turned and said to everyone, "Raise the red flag, start the singing!" And the heroic Steel Company's chorus began to ring out. The chorus drowned out the wind and the waves and the sound of the plane's engine.

121. The enemy plane flew off and the soldiers said it had gone to announce the funeral. Steel Company escort squadron, made up of ten armed fishing boats, followed Boat 1 into the center channel. There was still no signal from the enemy ships and this was a source of considerable anxiety on board.

122. Commander Ding was also worrying about the nonappearance of the enemy ships. At this moment he was going over the problem with his chief of operations, Du, on board the flagship.

123. Commander Ding raised his binoculars and spotted a searchlight in the distance and he knew the enemy had arrived. "Order the escort squadron to meet them and lead the enemy ships off our course," he commanded, and the chief of operations immediately relayed the order.

124. On receiving the order, Xiao Ding shouted, "Ready for battle!" and the trumpeter sounded the call to arms. The engine was started and they surged forward toward the enemy.

125. Just at this critical point the wind suddenly dropped. The old fisherman Jin Da-yi reported to Commander Ding and said that there would be no more wind for another three or four hours. At this moment, they should do everything they could to get across the center channel as quickly as possible. For if they did not, now that the wind had stopped, the current would carry them in the direction of the enemy.

126. Soon after the flagship had dropped its sail, the boom of enemy guns was borne across the water and the sound of enemy planes could be heard above as they came in to start bombing the fleet.

127. Commander Ding thought deeply for a while and then made his decision. He ordered all troops and officers to use paddles, oars, spades, rifle butts, even their bare hands to row across the center channel.

128. Just as Commander Ding was issuing this order, Xiao Ding's boat was surrounded by the salvos fired from the enemy ships. The boat had received several minor hits and the soldiers used their knapsacks and jackets to plug up the holes, but no sooner had they blocked them than the stormy sea brought water cascading in again.

129. Commander Ding asked Xiao Ding over the walkie-talkie what the situation was. Xiao Ding reported that the situation was not good, but that no matter what the difficulties they could still undertake their battle tasks.

130. Just as Commander Ding was about to reply, the chief of operations handed him a telegram. He took one look and immediately switched on all transmitters to announce, "Soldiers, officers, comrades! Chairman Mao has cabled to ask if we can make land on time. . . ."

131. When this message reached Xiao Ding's boat, the No. 2 Squad leader excitedly shouted into the transmitter, "Please ask Chairman Mao not to worry! We guarantee to make land on time!" This message was sent not only from one boat but simultaneously from all the boats in the fleet!

132. Commander Ding ordered the escort squadron immediately to mount an attack on the enemy's rearguard. Then pointing to the cable pad, he said to the chief of operations, "Send a report to the Chairman—the soldiers have asked him not to worry. We shall definitely make land on time!"

133. As soon as he received the commander's order, Xiao Ding inspected his boat and ordered the soldiers to cut down the sail and shrouds and also to redouble their efforts to stop up the holes and bail out the water.

134. Borne forward by the swell, Xiao Ding's boat slowly approached the enemy's ship "Taihua." The comrades on the boat had all prepared their life-saving equipment and put five ten-kilo packages of high explosives in the bow.

135. Xiao Ding shook hands with each of the soldiers in turn and last of all with Xiao Hong. He ordered everybody to abandon ship and the soldiers held on to his hand as they wished Xiao Ding and the No. 2 Squad leader success in their attempt to blow up the "Taihua."

136. Xiao Ding and the No. 2 Squad leader were now alone on the boat. The No. 2 Squad leader held a coiled rope with a grappling hook fastened to the end of it and stood in the bow; Xiao Ding was at the stern using the rudder as an oar. They silently came up to the "Taihua."

137. When the fishing boat touched the rear port side of the "Taihua" in the darkness, the No. 2 Squad leader threw up the rope with the grappling hook and with a crack it fastened on to the rail of the enemy ship. The No. 2 Squad leader pulled on the rope to tie up the boat against the ship's side.

138. As bad luck would have it, the noise of the grappling hook landing on the "Taihua's" rail had been heard by a guard. The guard shouted, "The Communists are alongside!" The No. 2 Squad leader immediately shot him.

139. With one hand gripping his gun and the other gripping the rail, the No. 2 Squad leader leaped aboard the enemy ship. He took up his position in front of the grappling hook and shouted, "Company Leader—set the fuse!"

140. Several dozen enemy sailors dashed toward the No. 2 Squad leader and he shot at them; some fell but the remainder came on. Lighting the fuse, Xiao Ding shouted to the No. 2 Squad leader, "Quick, jump into the sea!"

141. Badly wounded, his ammunition exhausted, the No. 2 Squad leader used his last remaining strength and, grappling with one of the enemy, jumped into the sea. Xiao Ding heard the No. 2 Squad leader shouting again, "Company Leader, blow it up!"

142. Hot tears swelled in his eyes as he said under his breath: "Comrade. . . ." and then he furiously lit the fuse and dived into the sea.

143. There was a huge explosion and a tremendous flash on the "Taihua." The roaring seas were lit up by a tremendous fire. The snake's head had been chopped off!

144. Following the destruction of the enemy's largest vessel, the remainder beat a disorderly retreat. When the bandit general heard that the "Taihua" had been destroyed and that Ai Dehua had been killed in the explosion, his face turned white as a sheet and he hurriedly boarded a transport plane and ran off to Taiwan.

145. By dawn our army had already set foot on Hainan. Xiao Ding led a party of soldiers as they landed and victoriously charged forward. Hainan Island was liberated!

LI SHUANGSHUANG

Size 12.5 x 10 cm

Original story by Li Jun

Adapted by He You-zhi

*Published by the Shanghai People's Art
    Publishing Co., Shanghai, 1964*

1. Sun Xiwang was well known in the village as a good
fellow; he had never caused anyone any embarrassment
and everyone said he was a regular guy. On this day he
was returning from the reservoir work site with Er Chun
and some others and boasting about his old woman as
they walked along.

2. Er Chun kidded him, "Elder Brother Xiwang, everybody
knows your wife waits on you hand and foot!" Xiwang
replied in a self-satisfied tone, "While the commune has
been so busy repairing the irrigation works, I've worn
out all my old shoes, but as soon as one pair wears out,
she's already made a new pair. And there's nothing special about that. My wife and I have always been like that.
I'm not joking."

3. Er Chun quickly said, "That shows how capable your wife is and is nothing for you to boast about." Xiwang shook his head, "What do you understand? If a man can't get his wife to do what he wants, what sort of a fellow is that?" Er Chun snorted, "That's feudal thinking, it's no good!"

4. As they were talking, a child suddenly came dashing up and shouted, "Uncle Xiwang, your wife is having a shouting match with Sun Youpo in the street!"

5. "Huh," sighed Xiwang as he left Er Chun and ran off toward the village street.

6. There was a crowd of people gathered on the street. Sun Youpo was shouting and gesticulating and Li Shuangshuang, holding back her anger, was asking in an accusing tone why she wanted to steal the team's barrel wood.

7. Xiwang broke into the group and tugged at Shuang-shuang. "Enough said, stop getting on the bad side of people! Let's go home." Shuangshuang paid no attention but pointing at Sun Youpo continued to expose her, and the more she spoke, the more furious she became.

8. Sun Youpo was fairly hopping with rage and shouting, when by good fortune her husband Sun You came by and dragged his better half away. As she left, Sun Youpo continued to curse Li Shuangshuang over her shoulder.

9. Shuangshuang wanted to go after her but Xiwang firmly held her back. "That's enough out of you. There aren't all that many pieces of barrel wood here!" Shuang-shuang angrily replied, "That may sound reasonable, but if everyone stole like her, there would not be enough to go around."

10. So saying, she gathered up the barrel slats and hur-ried off to the carpenter's team.

11. Xiwang quickly went back home. The door was pad-locked and there were several sentences chalked up on it: "Key is in usual place. Xiao Ju is at her auntie's home. When you get back, first light the fire."

12. As soon as Xiwang saw the words "When you get back, first light the fire," he felt even more angry. He immediately ripped down the penciled note, took the key from the window ledge, opened the door, and stormed into the room, going straight over to lie down on the **kang.**

13. It was already noon and still Shuangshuang had not returned. Xiwang was very hungry and was just thinking of getting up when he heard someone at the door and Shuangshuang came in, leading their daughter Xiao Ju.

14. Xiwang quickly lay down again and turned his face to the wall. Shuangshuang took no notice of him but handed Xiao Ju a cold steamed bread roll and told her to go outside.

15. Next she raked out the stove and looked into the cooking pot. There was no water in it and she said angrily, "When you came home, why didn't you rake out the stove and put on the water and get a move on! . . ."

16. Xiwang abruptly sat up. "I can't accept this tyranny. If I start cooking for you, next thing I'll be washing your underpants!" Shuangshuang was furious. "You don't seem to be doing much while here I am as busy as anything; haven't you got eyes in your head?"

17. So saying, Shuangshuang began slicing the noodles. Xiwang jumped off the **kang** and said, "That's your own fault! You're an activist, but who gives you anything for that?"

18. The more Shuangshuang listened, the more impatient she became. Stamping her foot, she slapped the knife down on the table and said, "Eat it, you won't like it!"

19. While Shuangshuang angrily sat on the sill wiping the tears from her eyes, Xiwang began to feel better and picking up the already sliced noodles said, "This is enough for me. I'll cook it myself."

20. He took two cloves of garlic and began to pound them with a mortar. The more Shuangshuang cried, the louder Xiwang pounded, and then Shuangshuang became really angry. She jumped up and began pummeling Xiwang on his back with her two fists.

21. "Right, you are rebelling against your husband," muttered Xiwang and he took off one of his shoes to beat her; but Shuangshuang grabbed him by his wrist and said, "Let's go. We'll ask the Party branch secretary to adjudicate!"

22. At mention of going to see the Party secretary, Xiwang knew that he would come off worse, so he quickly broke free and leaped out through the gateway, turning to shout, "Let's go. You follow me; I'll go first!" and then he dashed off back to work.

23. By evening Xiwang had not returned home. After eating supper, Shuangshuang put the child to bed and sat alone by the window, sewing the sole of a shoe. She was thinking about her argument with Xiwang and also about why the production spirit of the women was so low.

24. Suddenly there was a slight cough at the door and somebody walked in. Shuangshuang, thinking it was Xiwang, did not turn to look, but it was in fact the wife of the team leader, You Fang.

25. You Fang's wife knew that the two of them had been arguing and said persuasively, "Call it a day! There's a proverb: 'A young couple bears no malice after an argument, for by day they eat from the same pot and at night they share the same pillow!'" Shuangshuang couldn't help smiling. "But we can't even eat together!"

26. Shuangshuang said, "You see, he's gone running off to take an active part in the irrigation works. If irrigation is so important, why are we buried at home?" You Fang's wife said to her, "My mother-in-law has been ticking me off again. She says there's absolutely no point in going. We don't get any extra work points so what's the point in going there and working like an ox?"

27. They were chatting merrily away when they heard someone giggling at the window. It was Sun Youpo's daughter, Gui Ying.

28. Gui Ying had just left lower middle school, and Shuangshuang was her best friend. Smiling, she came in and said, "Same with me. My mother often says to me, 'Why don't you hurry up and go to the town and find work there. There's no point in taking part in the labor here.' You must agree, that talk is pretty unpleasant!"

29. Why did none of the households send their women out to work? Shuangshuang felt that it was connected with the fact that the recording of work points was slack. As soon as she brought this up, You Fang's wife added, "Yes, and it's Assistant Team Leader Jin Qiao who is to blame for doing away with the recording of work points; in other villages they still make settlements to everyone —according to their work points!"

30. Shuangshuang slapped her thigh. "Ha, didn't the Party secretary say the other day that everybody should express their opinions? Let's bring this out and write a big-character poster!" When You Fang's wife and Gui Ying heard the idea of putting up a big-character poster, they began to hesitate; one said she couldn't write characters and the other said she feared a scolding from her grandfather.

31. Shuangshuang boldly said, "I'll write it. This matter is too important to be passed over!" And You Fang's wife added, "That's for sure. As soon as work points are issued according to the work done, whoever is free will want to go and win some points." They all smiled.

32. Two days later, early in the morning in the most striking position in the village street, a big-character poster appeared. Although the characters were not written too well, the content was fresh and lively and it instantly aroused everybody's interest:

Big-character Poster

The harvest is over and the sickles have been put away; now the irrigation works are being repaired and the fields are being planted. There isn't enough labor to go around, but the women stay at home with nothing to do. Why is there a shortage of people going out to join the labor force? It's all because the cadres are lazy so the work points are recorded slackly. Don't you know who is the work-point recorder? I hope he will hurry up and start recording work points. The women can work half the day.

Li Shuangshuang

33. Just at this moment Secretary Liu of the commune committee, the Party secretary, and You Fang were passing by. When Secretary Liu had read the big-character poster, he said to You Fang, "An excellent criticism! This is an important problem in your team. I think you should do some research into it straightaway."

34. Secretary Liu then asked, "Li Shuangshuang . . . whose wife is that?" The former secretary You Fang was not too certain but thought it was the wife of Xiwang. They asked around and someone explained that it was Xiwang's wife and that Li Shuangshuang was the new name she had chosen for herself when she had gone to the people's school the previous year.

35. While they were discussing this, Xiwang arrived on his way back from the work site, pushing a wheelbarrow. When everyone saw him they shouted, "Xiwang, come over here! Was this big-character poster written by your old woman or not?"

36. Xiwang got quite a fright as he thought to himself, "Let's hope it's not the business of my argument which has come out!" He was in something of a panic as he read the big-character poster, humphing all the while, and it was only when he had read it through that he felt relieved.

37. Secretary Liu said to the branch secretary, "This big-character poster is well written." Turning around, Xiwang said with a smile, "Uncle Progressive, the poster was written by the woman in my house."

38. No sooner had he said this than they all burst out laughing. Xiwang thought they were laughing at him because they thought he was boasting, so he quickly tried to explain. "What? Really it was she who wrote it! That one that cooks for me can write. Not only does she write big-character posters but she also writes lots of little-character posters in the house!"

39. Secretary Liu said with a smile, "Young man, in the future you must change your old habits; how can you still call your wife 'the woman in my house' or 'the one that cooks for me'? And as for the small-character posters only appearing inside your house, surely that's slightly undemocratic." Only half understanding, Xiwang began laughing again.

40. It never occurred to Xiwang that the Secretary of the Party Committee of the Commune would attach such importance to the poster. When he got home he sat looking at Shuangshuang, laughing and giggling at her. Shuangshuang began to lose her patience and finally said, "So you've decided to come back to eat, have you?"

41. It was only then that Xiwang said seriously, "Mother of Xiao Ju, you're no fool! Writing a big-character poster for Commune Secretary Liu to see. He said your opinions were extremely good and that the commune committee would have to do special research into the whole matter." Both happy and worried, Shuangshuang asked, "Are you sure? Is that really true?"

42. Smiling from ear to ear, Xiwang said, "How could it be otherwise? If you really can go to earn a few work points, from now on I'll give you a hand with the food."

43. Xiwang thought for a moment and added, "But in the future, you shouldn't just write the first thing that comes into your head. You know what policy means. If you write any old nonsense, washing our dirty linen in public, then what are we to do?"

44. Shuangshuang's eyebrows shot up as she said, "You must be a coward. The Party leadership saw the poster today, so what are you afraid of? If there is something on one's mind, one should tell it to the Party. I can't stand the type of person who every time he rakes out the cinders is frightened of burning himself."

45. On the next day the team called a commune members' meeting. The Party branch secretary, holding up a work-point book, said a few words. "From today, we want to record work points conscientiously. As I see it, this should help cure some people's faults." As he said this, he fixed his eye on Sun Youpo.

46. Everyone began to join in a lively discussion. Some nominated Gui Ying, others Shuangshuang. At this point Sun Youpo stood up and said, "It's no small matter to be work-point recorder. It should be someone friendly. I think Xiwang fits the bill!"

47. Assistant Team Leader Jin Qiao quickly seconded him. Several people also said, "Yes, let's choose Xiwang." Xiwang quickly stepped forward and said, "I couldn't do this job. I can't write account figures, nor can I use an abacus. I would muddle everybody's points, so how could I possibly take it on?"

48. Suddenly Shuangshuang jumped up. "He can keep accounts and he can write account figures—he taught me!" Seeing that she had let the cat out of the bag, Xiwang embarrassedly said, "Stop talking! There's no need for you to say any more! When did I ever teach you to write account figures!"

49. Shuangshuang pointed a finger directly at him. "This spring! Do you dare deny it? Whether or not he's done something to distinguish himself, we'll never drag this donkey along. The more you try to force him, the more stubborn he gets."

50. Seeing that Xiwang was speechless, You Fang found a way out of the impasse by saying, "All right—if Xiwang really isn't willing, how about electing Shuangshuang?" Xiwang got a terrific shock and hurriedly said, "What? Let her do it? That . . . I'm still a bit better than her. Let me do it."

51. The meeting ended with roars of laughter. The Party branch secretary handed over the pile of work-point books to Xiwang. Seeing that everybody was taking the matter of work-point books very seriously, without realizing it, he regained his composure, rolled up his sleeves, and called everybody to come and collect their books.

52. He carefully wrote the owner's name on each work-point book as he gave them out to everyone. Shuangshuang also received one and the ever-quarrelsome Sun Youpo and Da Feng, who were rarely seen in the fields, also grabbed theirs.

53. Xiwang worked for a long time before he had finished handing out the work-point books and when he returned home he stood in the doorway and let out a long sigh.

54. Shuangshuang smilingly said, "Hello! What's the matter with you?" Xiwang slapped his head with his hand several times. "Ugh! I feel as if I'm coming apart. I'm tired out. I'm no good for this brain work!"

You haven't written yet! Even though the pen is very small. as soon as you pick it up, it feels as heavy as a shovel.

What idiotic talk. I've written characters, too, you know. When I become work recorder, I won't write as messily as you.

Once you have a good name, you should live up to it; there's no one in the village can say that I don't. My father, my grandfather . . .

I won't listen, I won't listen! You are going to recite your family tree again and say that for generations your family has never argued with anyone.

55. Shuangshuang caught sight of his hand as he stretched to take a drink and said, "Hm. People usually write characters on paper—how come you write them on your hand!"

56. Xiwang washed his hands, swallowed hard, and said, "You know, if you're the work-points recorder you have to be making apologies to everyone all the time." Shuangshuang didn't agree. "How come? Depending on how much work someone does, you just record the points. If you set it up right and keep it going strictly without bias, who can say anything against you?"

57. Xiwang was somewhat dejected. Shuangshuang urged him to put the public good before his own while working for the masses, to conscientiously put into operation the work-point system and then there would certainly be a lot of people turning out to join the work. When Xiwang remembered that Sun Youpo and Da Feng had also just taken work-point books, he couldn't help nodding in agreement.

58. That very day the team put into operation the system of work assignments and work points. Xiwang, Sun You, and several others undertook the work of spreading manure on eight **mu** of freshly planted wheat. Because the manure was some distance from the field they had to fetch it as well as spread it. Sun You kept muttering as he carried the manure.

59. Just at this moment Jin Qiao came along. As soon as he saw the manure they had laid on the field he asked, "Still so much to do! How much have you spread?" Sun You looked very displeased. "It's a big field. The tools are not up to much. We certainly got the worst of it when we undertook to do this work."

60. Just at this moment an empty truck came by. Jin Qiao immediately recognized the driver as Xiao Wang, a long-distance truck driver, and waving and shouting, he ran to the road. "Xiao Wang, where are you going? Stop and have a rest—have a drink of water."

61. The truck stopped at the side of the road beside the pile of manure. Jin Qiao poured out a bowl of water and led Xiao Wang to a shady spot and began chatting. Sun You came up behind the truck and took a look and thought to himself that if the driver would help, they could have the manure spread in no time.

62. He then told this excellent idea to Jin Qiao who said, with some embarrassment, as soon as he'd thought it over, "Right away! Xiao Wang, how about bringing the manure to the field on the truck for us?" At first Xiao Wang was unwilling, but later he was unable to withstand Jin Qiao's mixture of pleading and threats; he could only agree.

63. They had the manure on the truck in no time. The truck slowly drove around the field. Sun You and the others stood on the back scattering the manure.

64. The assigned eight **mu** were completed in the twinkling of an eye. Sun You and the rest took out their work-point books for Xiwang to mark in the work points. Xiwang generously recorded ten points for each of them, even putting ten points down in Sun You's book.

65. At this moment Shuangshuang and the other women were in the cotton fields deciding on their work points. Finally they came to Da Feng, and Sun Youpo was the first to express an opinion. "She spent the whole afternoon clearing up six rows. Give her five points."

66. "I don't agree!" interrupted Shuangshuang immediately. "We shouldn't only take into account speed, but also consider quality." So saying, she pointed to a row of cotton flowers. "Look, she did those rows without getting rid of all the weeds, which means that later on there will be fewer bolls!"

67. One of the team members came forward to solve the situation. "Give four points!" "Four points is all right," said Shuangshuang, "as long as she comes back in the afternoon to do the rows over again." Da Feng couldn't restrain her anger. "I don't need the work points—I've still got my parents!" and turning on her heel, she left.

68. Neither Gui Ying nor You Fang's wife were content with Da Feng and they hurriedly returned home to eat. Shuangshuang was furious as she stayed behind to redo the rows which Da Feng had done.

69. When she had finished she set off for home, and on the way she passed the wheat field where she saw old Gengpo, who was plowing and grumbling to himself, "Ha! Is this supposed to be a job of work? I've never seen anything like it!" Shuangshuang stopped to ask what the trouble was.

70. Shuangshuang glanced over the field and asked, "Who was it who spread the manure?" Old Gengpo snorted, "Who? You'll know when you get home!" Shuangshuang asked no more questions but hurried back to the village.

71. When she got to the village street, she ran into Xiwang who was bringing Xiao Ju to meet her. As soon as he saw her, Xiwang, full of smiles, asked, "Knocked off so late? Busy half the day? How many work points did you get?" Shuangshuang said, "Five points. And you?"

72. Xiwang laughed and said, self-satisfied, "You're asking about us? Well, Sun You, in no more time than it takes to smoke a few pipes, had earned ten points and as for Jin Qiao, with a few strokes of his spade he had also earned ten points." Shuangshuang questioned him further and discovered that their assigned work was none other than the field which Old Gengpo was plowing.

73. Xiwang had no idea that Shuangshuang was angry and he continued to put on airs. "That's why they say if you want to earn work points, you have to be smart in choosing the work you do. It's written in the disappointed look in your eyes!" He hadn't finished when Shuangshuang broke in with a change of mood. "You really know how to cheat—working without a thought for the quality of the work! That won't do!"

74. She shook her head and, with a snort, ran into the house and furiously took up the brush which was on the table and started quickly writing characters on a sheet of paper.

75. Xiwang followed her in to see what she was doing and saw that she had written several rows of large characters: "Some of the commune members are not so good; they don't take work points seriously, paying no attention to quality but just taking into account speed, doing their work opportunistically." Xiwang said shocked, "You. . . . You're writing a big-character poster again?"

76. Shuangshuang said bitterly, "I won't tolerate spreading manure like that, and I won't tolerate clearing up the cotton stems like that either." Xiwang was so upset he started shifting from foot to foot. "You're always poking your nose in other people's affairs; you'll get yourself into trouble."

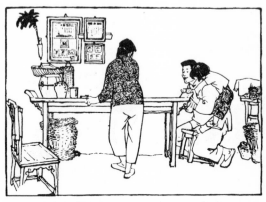

77. He whipped out some work-point tickets and said, "If you think you earned too few work points today, I'll give you two of mine." Shuangshuang pushed his hand away. "I'm not after your work points. It is not work points I'm after at all.

78. Xiwang pleaded with her, "Mother of Xiao Ju, I'm involved in this. Even if they took more work points than they should have, I was the work-point recorder. I wasn't going to record the extra points but they began to kick up a fuss and I got all confused."

79. Shuangshuang was so angry that she began to tremble all over. "If you hadn't been involved in this, I would have exposed it in a big-character wall poster, but since it does involve you, I'll go to the commune to accuse you." So saying, she threw down her pen and like a gust of wind rushed out of the house.

80. She reached the commune office in no time and reported the whole thing to Secretary Liu. He said with a smile, "This includes Xiwang. Isn't he your husband?"

81. Shuangshuang explained, "My husband has no sense of right or wrong and he has no definite principles and he's easily swayed. But Sun You is not like that; he's full of bad ideas. He's not a member of the proletariat. Our family is."

82. Secretary Liu now understood everything. He asked Shuangshuang what she thought was the best way to guarantee quality. Shuangshuang did not know. He said, "For example, we should strengthen political education as well as making sure that assignments are properly fulfilled. What do you think of that?" Shuangshuang nodded in full agreement.

83. Secretary Liu also asked Shuangshuang whether she was a woman cadre. She shook her head. "No, people said my tongue was too sharp." Secretary Liu smiled and said, "If you are impartial and genuinely responsible, your tongue should be sharp. But at the same time, if something comes up we should consult with the masses."

84. The next day, the Party branch secretary called a meeting of all the team members near the field of wheat stubble. Sun You, Jin Qiao, and Xiwang all made a self-criticism and the secretary said, "Let's consider the matter now closed. In the future we should put into operation the system of group responsibility."

85. The Party secretary continued, "Today our team has to elect a women's team leader. The Party branch opinion is to let Li Shuangshuang try it. What does everyone think of that?" No sooner had he finished than everybody at the meeting raised their hands and shouted, "Agreed! Agreed!"

86. Everybody wanted Shuangshuang to say what she thought, but she only smiled to herself and refused. The branch secretary said, "In that case, I'll say something. Since we elected Shuangshuang, from now on we must listen to her instructions and that applies especially to us men laborers."

87. The Party branch secretary faced Shuangshuang and said, "As for you, Shuangshuang, you must also take great care." Xiwang glanced quickly at Shuangshuang and she pouted her lips at him and everybody exploded into laughter.

88. After the meeting had broken up, Xiwang followed behind Shuangshuang, embarrassed and silent.

89. On the way, Shuangshuang suddenly discovered a pig eating the maize. She picked up a stone and cried out, "Shoo!" and ran off to chase the pig away. Xiwang, startled, raised his head and saw Jin Qiao walking along the path alone, his head lowered.

90. Xiwang ran up to Jin Qiao and quietly offered his apologies. Jin Qiao nonchalantly said, "What Shuangshuang proposed was correct and I accept it. However, Xiwang, old fellow, you should keep a rein on that wife of yours. If she carries on like this, she will step on everybody's toes in the village."

91. These words of Jin Qiao struck home. Xiwang hurriedly said, "Of course, of course, you just wait and see. If I can't tame her this time, then I'll . . . I'll. . . ." He swallowed hard and ran off.

92. When Xiwang got home, Shuangshuang was discussing with old Gengpo the question of using animal power for the water wheel. She had her back to Xiwang and he coughed twice impatiently as he went in.

93. Shuangshuang turned around and said gently, "Are you back?" Xiwang put on a stern face. "Hm, team leader. Now that your public duties are over, could you come and do some private business for me?" Shuangshuang thought he was still joking and rolling her eyes at him said, "Oh, look at you."

94. Xiwang was completely serious. "Nobody's joking with you. Go and pack my things." Shuangshuang was suddenly worried. "What, are you going on a trip?" Xiwang stared at the ceiling. "Huh! I'm going to do transportation. I won't rot any more in this house."

95. Shuangshuang was stunned. Xiwang looked hard at her. "From now on our paths won't cross again. You will have fewer big-character posters to write and I will suffer less criticism. Even if you tread on everyone's toes, it won't be my responsibility."

96. Shuangshuang frowned deeply and looked at Xiwang sadly. All he did was to urge her to pack his things. But Shuangshuang did not appear to have heard. Xiwang angrily rolled up his sleeves and packed a blanket and a few clothes into a bundle.

97. Shuangshuang whipped the bundle away and said, "You can't go! Now that I'm team leader, I really need your help. Look at it from my point of view. I can't. . . ." She put her head on Xiwang's shoulder and began to cry.

98. Xiwang softened. "If I'm staying, we must establish a few rules." Surprisingly, Shuangshuang agreed.

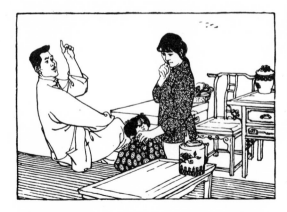

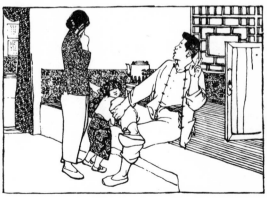

99. Pleased with himself, Xiwang sat down on the **kang,** crossed his legs, and said, "Now that you are a cadre, you must use your head before you open your mouth. Don't chatter like a machine gun. From now on, only say what you have to say and don't say anything you shouldn't." Shuangshuang nodded and said, "All right, that's one rule."

100. Raising a second finger, Xiwang said, "You are the leader of the women's team; just concern yourself with matters affecting production." Shuangshuang thought a bit and said, "That's all right as well; whatever happens I'll look after whatever I ought to do."

101. "As for the last rule, when you are dealing with people, give them some leeway and don't make so many proposals to the cadres. . . ." Before he had finished, Shuangshuang's expression suddenly changed and she snapped at him, "What?"

102. Unable to control her anger any more, Shuangshuang threw his bundle out of the door and said furiously, "Out you go!"

103. Originally Xiwang had only wanted to scare Shuang-shuang; he had had no idea that she would react like this. He picked up the bundle and stood there dumbly, waiting. After a long time he said slowly, "There's no need for you to be angry. Let's say there are only two rules. I'll never mention the third one, all right?"

104. But the domestic storm did not die down. The next day, the team committee held a meeting to discuss the distribution of extra points to needy households. After this matter had been dealt with, the chairman of the meeting, Jin Qiao, wanted to raise the question of cadres who needed extra work points because they couldn't spend all their time in production.

105. Shuangshuang's opinion was that cadres already had compensatory work points and therefore should not receive extra relief work points. But the team accountant thought otherwise. He said, "Compensatory and relief work points are two different things. Look at Xiwang's household, for example. Now that Shuangshuang is the team leader, it's bound to be affected."

I think we should be realistic. Look at Jin Qiao, for example; he's so busy every day that he doesn't even have time to go home and eat. I think we should give him several hundred relief work points.

106. Shuangshuang burst out, "My family should not be a candidate for relief. A cadre should also be engaged in production." Er Chun agreed with her and also thought that cadre families should not qualify for relief work points. The accountant, on seeing that his first point met with little response, proposed a second one.

107. Shuangshuang frowned and thought to herself, "The former branch secretary is busier than anybody else and he manages. Da Feng is young and unmarried—why can't she manage a living? If she can't, it's time she learned." She was just about to stand up to speak when Xiwang restrained her.

108. Jin Qiao wanted to avoid a stalemate so he craftily proposed that from then on he would do more labor. The team accountant, seeing the way things were going, joined in and said, "That's right. Whoever doesn't want to do labor work is a nobody. Shall we estimate Jin Qiao's household at several hundred work points?"

Us cadres have to be practical and realistic; we cannot allow the masses to point at us behind our backs. Two fat people just resting—of course they cannot receive work points!

109. Shuangshuang could not bear it any longer. She jumped up and Xiwang hurriedly kicked her again. Shuangshuang returned a fierce kick and said in a loud voice, "I still have something to say."

110. First she told them what she had been thinking and then she asked Jin Qiao why he didn't even pick up a spade or let his wife Da Feng go down to the fields. Jin Qiao lowered his head without a word and could think of nothing to say.

111. Xiwang tried to say a few words to resolve the impasse, but he was immediately rebuffed by Er Chun. Then, pulling at Shuangshuang's sleeve, Jin Qiao said, "All right, all right. After this, if I get work points, I'll eat, but if I don't get work points, I won't come to you!"

112. The meeting came to an unsatisfactory and unhappy conclusion. Xiwang looked at Shuangshuang angrily and pulled Jin Qiao into a corner to say something to him and then left the meeting furiously.

113. When Shuangshuang got home, she was startled to see that everything had been turned upside down in the house, and after a quick check she found that a blanket and a pillow were missing. Xiwang was gone.

114. Hurriedly she looked for him all over the village but with no success. She rushed to the cart depot and found out from old Gengpo that Xiwang had just left the village with Jin Qiao and Sun You on a cart.

115. She went to the edge of the village and saw the cart disappearing rapidly in the distance. She stared ahead of her, overwhelmed with grief.

116. It was dusk and the bell marking the end of the day's work was ringing. Shuangshuang went home and threw herself on the **kang**.

117. Just at this unhappy moment of grief the branch secretary came in.

118. He sat down with a sigh. "What's the matter? Has Xiwang left you?" Shuangshuang shook her head. "Life goes on. Even if this work-point recorder leaves me, I, as a cadre, still have work to do."

119. The branch secretary said, "Oh, never mind if they've gone. During the past few days they said they would start working in side occupations. But we must not slacken our efforts. Agriculture is the basis; the livelihood of the commune members comes from the land."

120. Shuangshuang nodded but, still unsettled, asked the branch secretary to judge who was right and who wrong. He said, "Your criticism of Jin Qiao was correct! Cadres should take part in production and in doing so lead production . . ."

121. After he had left, Shuangshuang thought to herself that any negligence in the work of the team could affect the livelihood of several hundred people and that she must never be slack herself but should bring the women together to get on well with their work. After eating supper she took Xiao Ju with her and went over to Jin Qiao's house.

122. Da Feng was crying at the side of the **kang.** She heard a noise at the door and saw that it was Shuangshuang. She gave her an angry glance and then quickly turned away. Sizing up the situation, Shuangshuang paused a second and then, plucking up her courage, went forward towards the **kang.**

123. Da Feng raised her head angrily and stared straight at Shuangshuang. "What have you come for? Aren't you content with driving my man away?" Shuangshuang shook her head and said gently, "No, I've come to see you. I tell you, Xiao Ju's father has also gone!"

124. When she heard this, Da Feng became more friendly and said with a sigh, "What's the use of pressing them so hard? Men are all the same; if you don't do as they say, they give up their family and run off."

125. Shuangshuang quickly turned the conversation onto the right track. "Da Feng, don't worry! We women have two hands as well! With them we can grow crops and cultivate cotton. Is it not right and glorious that we should eat the fruits of our labor and wear the clothes that we ourselves have produced?"

126. Then Da Feng, nodding, started to say what was on her mind. She said that it was not that she did not want to go down to the fields but that there were certain agricultural tasks she couldn't do. Shuangshuang saw that she had understood and quietly encouraged her. The two continued laughing and talking until late at night.

127. The more Shuangshuang went around to the women in their homes, the more they rallied round to follow her. On this particular day Shuangshuang bumped into Gui Ying just as she was leaving the office. Gui Ying held on to Shuangshuang's arm and said, "Auntie, I was just looking for you! Hurry up, hurry up!"

128. Shuangshuang hurriedly asked, "What's the matter? What's made you so flustered?" Gui Ying explained that her mother had told Jin Qiao to find a fiancé for her in the town and that today he was coming to ask her hand. Shuangshuang asked her what she intended to do about Er Chun. Gui Ying blushed. "I don't know."

129. "Silly, this is no time for hemming and hawing! Hurry up and say what you think of Er Chun." Shuangshuang began laughing and Gui Ying quickly replied, "I've never thought of him! How can you laugh when someone's in such a state? . . ."

130. Shuangshuang stopped laughing and said, "Really—what time does the man come?" Gui Ying said, "Right now!" Shuangshuang thought for a moment and then asked what his name was and then said, thinking aloud, "It looks as if I'd better go and see what's going on!"

131. She rushed straight off to Sun You's gateway. Sun Youpo, wearing new clothes and brilliant make-up, was standing by the gateway looking up and down waiting for somebody. As soon as she saw this scene, Shuangshuang realized that the prospective husband had not yet arrived and she quickly went on towards the edge of the village.

132. After a while a man appeared, coming along the main road, and asked an old woman the way. Shuangshuang heard that he was asking the way to Sun You's and guessed that it was the prospective husband. She called out, "Aren't you Xiao Wang, the truck driver?"

133. Xiao Wang, dressed in his best suit, responded with surprise and started to get uneasy. Shuangshuang smiled and said, "I knew you were going to come today!" Xiao Wang felt even more uneasy and was speechless for a long while before inquiring, "Ah, is auntie in good health?"

134. Shuangshuang asked, "You've come to get engaged, haven't you? Do you know Gui Ying?" Xiao Wang blushed and said, "I haven't met her yet but as soon as we meet, I'll know her. I'm a very open type of person."

135. Shuangshuang laughed and said, "I'm Gui Ying's aunt and Gui Ying has asked me to tell you that she doesn't know you, doesn't understand you, and moreover she's already got a fiancé in the village. . . ."

136. Xiao Wang looked as if a pail of cold water had been tipped over him, and Shuangshuang said, "Comrade, it's not your fault. It is Gui Ying's mother who wants to marry her to you so that you will take Gui Ying with you to live in the town." Xiao Wang waved his arm vigorously. "That's no good. Today marriage is freely entered into by principles!"

137. Shuangshuang then pressed him to go and see Gui Ying, but he hurriedly said, "Oh no, there's been a slight misunderstanding! Please tell Comrade Gui Ying that I wish to apologize to her." With this he left.

138. Not long after Xiao Wang had left, a cloud of dust appeared on the road outside the village and Jin Qiao, Sun You, and Xiwang, each driving a large cart, came hurrying into sight. When Xiwang saw the men and women all happily at work he couldn't help remembering his own worries.

139. The carts drew into the cart depot and old Gengpo helped them unharness the horses. Sun You and Jin Qiao both hurried off to their homes. Hugging his bundle, Xiwang hesitated a second and then, as if he had come to some decision, sat down.

140. Just at that moment Xiao Ju came running towards him, her arms held wide, shouting, "Papa!" He quickly threw his bundle to one side in order to hug Xiao Ju, and then he suddenly saw Shuangshuang standing by the gate watching him, her eyes wide open and her lips firmly pursed shut.

141. Many words surged through Xiwang's mind. He wanted to speak but his own pride held him back, so he put down the child and picked up his bundle again.

142. When Shuangshuang saw that he was about to walk off towards the stable, she ran forward and wrenched the bundle from his arms, saying, "I see your bundle is dirty. We are wiping out the four pests at the moment; it'll soon be the five pests, unless we get rid of you soon!" And she walked out of the depot.

143. Xiwang, embarrassed, was hesitating when old Gengpo gave him a shove and said, "Go home! Don't hang around here." Xiwang picked up Xiao Ju and dashed after Shuangshuang.

144. When he got to the gate of his own home he unexpectedly ran into her again. There was a large group of people in the courtyard surrounding Shuangshuang and Sun You was pointing an accusing finger while blurting out, "I've been waiting all this time! I've waited to this moment and who would have thought that you would have frightened our family's guest away! Breaking up somebody else's marriage is a wicked thing to do!"

145. Xiwang felt quite numb and couldn't budge an inch. He watched Shuangshuang say firmly, "That is not right. Gui Ying already has a fiancé. Now we have free choice in marriage; they can't be arranged any more. You can't only have your eyes fixed on the town. . . ."

146. Jin Qiao stared at Xiwang and then patted him on the arm, asking him to go outside for a few words around the corner. Xiwang was still standing irresolutely when Shuangshuang started arguing with Sun Youpo at the top of her voice.

147. Xiwang heard this and saw it all clearly: Shuangshuang had started meddling in the important matter of somebody else's marriage. He felt very angry, walked up to her, and said grimly, "I've had just about enough of you!" He grabbed his bundle and, without looking back, ran out of the gate.

148. Xiao Ju began crying and shouting "Papa!" and struggled to break free from Shuangshuang to run after him. Shuangshuang was absolutely furious and stood in front of her holding her tightly by the hand. Seeing the awkward situation, Sun You and his wife and Jin Qiao left.

149. Xiwang sat all night in the stable attached to the cart depot and planned to join Jin Qiao and Sun You the following day to drive the carts into the district town again.

150. As soon as it was light, Xiwang left without uttering a sound. It was the hottest part of summer and the heat was exhausting. After the carts had gone about five miles, the horses were covered in sweat and breathing heavily, so Jin Qiao, Xiwang, and the others unharnessed the horses to cool them with a drink at a shady, grassy spot by the river.

151. Jin Qiao suddenly discovered that there was a melon field not far from where they were. He went over to take a closer look and then shouted to the others, "Come over here, quick! Come over here! Come and eat some melons!"

152. The melons were just being harvested and were piled high. The three of them bought a large one and praised it as they ate. "Phew, this melon is really sweet!"

153. When the two men who were arranging the baskets of melons heard they were going to the town, they quickly asked, "You're going to town? What a stroke of luck; we've bought these melons but we were wondering how to get them to town since we have no transport! Could you take them to town for us?"

154. Jin Qiao asked them how much they were prepared to pay, and then took Xiwang and Sun You to one side and quietly began to discuss it with them. Sun You said, "As far as I'm concerned, let's take it on. As for the fee, there's no point in handing in a receipt; we'll just split it three ways and leave it at that!"

155. At first Xiwang felt that it would not be right to do this, but he was no match for the arguments of the other two and he finally gave up and said nothing more. But no matter what, he refused to accept his share of the fee. Once it was settled, the melons were loaded onto the carts.

156. Summer passed and autumn came; in the twinkling of an eye, two months had gone by. They had transported the last load of timber and driven the carts back into the district town and were feeding the horses at the transport station. Xiwang sat to one side staring down the street and dully started to think of his family.

157. Suddenly the sound of an approaching bicycle bell could be heard and Er Chun came riding into sight. As soon as he saw him, Xiwang happily jumped forward and shouted, "Er Chun! Er Chun! So you've come to town! What've you come to buy?"

158. Er Chun had come to town to buy some work-point books and had also brought some things for repair. Xiwang asked, "Is your family busy? How are our team's crops?"

159. Xiwang dragged Er Chun to one side and asked, "Your aunt hasn't been making trouble for people recently, has she?" Er Chun replied, "Ha! Made trouble! If she hadn't led the women through the mud and water, the crops wouldn't have grown as well as they have. All you have to do is go back and you'll see what I mean!"

160. On hearing this, Xiwang said, "I would never have thought it! . . ." Er Chun couldn't help laughing. "You would never have thought it? All you have to do is take a look. Come back soon, Aunt Shuangshuang is thinking of you!"

161. Laughing as he said this, Er Chun jumped on his bicycle and rode off.

162. After a few days, Jin Qiao and the others drove their carts back to the village. Just at the edge of the village they saw Shuangshuang leading a group of people. They were singing as they carried the freshly cut maize. The more they sang, the happier they were, and the further they went, the quicker they walked.

163. Seeing the lively scene on either side of the road and hearing laughter from every direction, Xiwang heaved a deep sigh and began to crack his whip in the air to speed home.

164. With a thunder of hoofs the horses turned in to the cart depot. When the carts had been put in position, Xiwang hurried off back home without waiting for old Gengpo's urging.

165. In a flash the news that the men who had been doing long-distance transport had returned was around the village. As soon as her work was finished, Shuangshuang quickly ran home.

166. She ran up to the gate and saw Xiwang splitting firewood with the big ax. He was putting tremendous force behind each blow as if all the trouble and shame of the last few months were being dispersed in one fell swoop.

167. "Mama, mama! Papa's come back!" shouted Xiao Ju as soon as she caught sight of her mother. Xiwang looked up and as soon as he saw that it was Shuangshuang, he involuntarily lowered his head.

168. Shuangshuang picked up Xiao Ju and said quietly to Xiwang, "The family can't do without you!" Xiwang could not say a word.

There's nothing to be ashamed of! We stay at home and work at agriculture and you go out of the village to work at side occupations. Both increase the team's income, don't they?

Coming back this time and finding that you had made such a good job of the crops, I just don't know what to say.

169. That night when Xiao Ju was fast asleep, Shuang-shuang took out a new pair of cotton shoes and handed them to Xiwang. "Put them on and see if they fit." Xiwang put them on, looked at his new shoes and then at Shuang-shuang, and smiled simply and honestly.

170. Shuangshuang sighed softly. "You fellows, as soon as you're out of the door you stay away several months . . . but as for us, not a day passed without our going to the edge of the village to see if you were returning!" Xiwang, staring at his new shoes, replied, "Don't say any more. I feel very bad about it. I want to apologize to you all!"

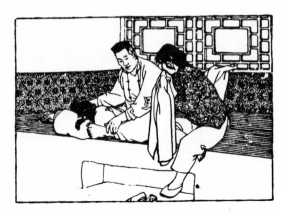

171. Shuangshuang's words struck home and Xiwang was lost in thought. Then he hesitantly asked, "Say, how long does it take before a man can finally get rid of his selfishness?" Shuangshuang replied, "That depends on how fast he raises his political consciousness; I guess there are quite a few people now who are not very selfish."

172. Xiwang shook his head. "It's not as simple as that; I've seen people who are still selfish stealthily making a profit out of the public." Shuangshuang realized that there was more to this than met the eye, and rather than offend him, she simply smiled and said, "Who stealthily makes a profit out of the public good?"

173. Xiwang was silent for a moment but in the end could not help but tell her how Jin Qiao and Sun You had transported the melons and divided the proceeds privately between themselves. Shuangshuang could not hide her irritation and shouted, "Huh! While the others were working their guts out at home, that's the sort of thing you were doing outside the village!"

174. Xiwang hurriedly explained that he himself had had no part in it, but Shuangshuang harshly asked, "If you only look after your own actions and pay no attention to those of others, are you a commune member? We produce collectively—even a single blade of grass has all our sweat on it!"

175. At this Xiwang began to sweat all over. "Well, well, what am I supposed to do about it?" Shuangshuang said, "Do? Do the same as I did! Put up a big-character poster!"

176. The next day, a new big-character poster appeared in the village street.

Big-character Poster

Uncle Sun You and younger brother Jin Qiao! Xiwang is not going to mince words with you today. It is not right. I can't go on covering for you about the business of the melons. If you don't make a clean breast of it, I'm going to bring it out into the open.

Sun Xiwang

People gathered in front of it and began discussing it. Some said, "Oh, another fresh scandal is coming out!" Others said, "Ugh, Xiwang can express opinions too!"

177. The big-character poster had not been up long before the branch secretary found Xiwang to hear about the situation. As they were talking about it, Jin Qiao came running along and grasped the branch secretary by the hand. "Old Uncle Progressive, I'm covered with shame! I was wrong, wrong! I confess to the organization. . . ."

178. Jin Qiao then admitted their corruption. Xiwang felt a bit uneasy and so he said, "Younger Brother Jin Qiao, I exposed you for your own good. You probably loathe me for it but that's up to you! From now on I'm going to speak out!"

179. The branch secretary said warmly to Jin Qiao, "If you've done something wrong you must be brave enough to admit it. You'll have to return the money and also explain to the commune members what has happened!" Jin Qiao looked thankfully at Xiwang and Xiwang no longer felt uneasy.

180. He left the branch secretary's home feeling very happy and caught sight of Er Chun who was waving a newspaper. "Er Chun," he shouted, "what's happened?" Er Chun pointed to a photograph in the paper and asked, "Do you recognize who this is?"

181. Xiwang jumped forward and glanced at it and then cried out in surprise, "It's your aunt Shuangshuang! She's in the paper!" "Yes," said Er Chun, his eyes wide. "Our production team's hard work, the successful operating of each according to his work, the excellent harvest, it's all in the paper!"

182. Xiwang said, "Ah, I was worried before about her quick tongue stirring up trouble, but now I know for sure what a good type she is!" Er Chun said, "Don't people also call you a 'good type'?" Xiwang threw back his head. "Me? I'm an old style 'good type'; she's a new style 'good type.' Politics takes command in the new style!"

183. "Er Chun, what tricks are you playing on your stupid uncle this time?" The two turned and saw that it was Shuangshuang. Er Chun, jumping up, said, "Aunt, you ask Xiwang—he was just boasting about how beautiful you'd become!"

184. Shuangshuang wanted to box his ears but Er Chun ran off with a laugh. She asked Xiwang what he had been bragging about. Xiwang thought for a long while and then mumbled, "Ah, I said that you were beautiful, and that's the truth! You've really become both clever and beautiful!"

185. Shuangshuang gave him a playful punch and smiled. "I'm not beautiful and I've got to spend the rest of my life with you!" Xiwang replied with unexpected seriousness, "As for me, one life time with you is not enough. It should be two!"

HOT ON THE TRAIL

Size 12.5 x 10 cm
Original story by An Zhong-min and Zhu Xiang-chun
Adapted by Xin Sheng
Drawings by Hao Shi
Published by the Shanghai People's Art Publishing Co., Shanghai, 1965

1. It is the end of September 1961 and a large party of overseas Chinese and Hong Kong Chinese are crossing the border at Shumchun to return to celebrate National Day. As they step on the soil of their fatherland and hear the loud-speakers say "Welcome to you returning to take part in the construction of the fatherland and welcome to you sight-seeing and visiting," they feel extremely elated.

2. At the customs post a woman customs officer is searching an old lady's bag. She finds a tin of cigarettes and, thinking it a bit odd, obtains the permission of the traveler to open it.

3. The customs officer tears open the cigarettes one by one and finds a detonator; on searching the bag again she finds a packet of gunpowder disguised as a packet of crystallized fruit. At first the old lady is dumbstruck and then, shaking her head, she denies that the bag is hers.

4. The officer takes the old lady to the head of the post and tells him, "The old lady insists these things are not hers and says that her bag was exchanged for somebody else's at the station." After a moment's thought, the head of the post sends the customs officer to the station to fetch Li Ming-gang, the Canton-based public security officer stationed at Shumchun.

5. Li Ming-gang is helping a woman traveler with her children and luggage. The customs officer says to him, "Comrade Li Ming-gang, the head of the customs post asks you to come." Li Ming-gang replies by seeing the traveler to the waiting room and sets off immediately.

6. Arriving at the customs post, Li Ming-gang sees an old lady sobbing as she says to the head of the post, "I came on the train from Hong Kong and somebody secretly exchanged my bag for another. When I looked inside the bag I found, in addition to the original contents, a gold chain as well as cigarettes and crystallized fruit and I wanted to keep them . . . I never thought what bad luck it would bring me!"

7. Li Ming-gang, having understood the facts of the matter, asks the old lady, "What did your own bag have in it?" She replies, "A few clothes, a couple of biscuits, a flannel bag, and also a child's toy car."

8. The head of the post says to the lady, "We certainly don't let bad people go free, nor do we imprison good people; there's nothing to worry about." Having calmed the old lady, he is just about to start analyzing the matter with Li Ming-gang, when suddenly a member of the station staff comes in with an unclaimed bag.

9. Li Ming-gang opens the bag and finds inside it clothes, two biscuits, a child's toy car, and everything else the old lady had said was in her bag. Li says to the head of the post, "As I see it, the enemy was using a switch bag technique to let someone else bring in the gunpowder for him. Knowing that it had been discovered, he discarded the old lady's bag."

10. The customs chief takes a careful look at the toy car and says, "This type of toy has an import tax, and the tax form will have the owner's name. All we have to do is check each of the passengers who brought in a toy car and then we will certainly find the guy who switched the bags."

11. Li Ming-gang calls the tax official and she checks through the tax form. Then she hands Li a list of the names and addresses of those who had brought in toy cars that day.

12. The head of the customs post rings up the Bureau of Public Security in Canton and asks them to find out which of the sixteen people on the list have not brought toy cars with them. The Bureau rings back after investigating to say that all sixteen have toy cars.

13. The head of the customs post puts down the receiver and after a moment of deep thought says, "If the person who switched the bags also thought that he could be traced through the tax form, is it not possible that he might have bought a similar toy car in Canton to cover up for the missing one?" "Very possible," says Li. "I'll go straight back to Canton to investigate."

14. As soon as he gets back to Canton, Li Ming-gang goes straight to the largest department store on the west bank.

15. In the children's toy department, Li Ming-gang sees a woman customer buying a battery-operated car. It is exactly the same as the toy car he has brought with him from Shumchun.

16. After some hesitation he takes out the car and asks the shop assistant's opinion. The assistant takes a look at it and says, "Yes, this one of yours was bought abroad."

17. The shop assistant explains to him, "The new toy cars made in Canton automatically turn away when they come into contact with an object, but the imported ones just stop." While explaining, he gives Li a demonstration so that he understands the difference.

18. Li Ming-gang returns to the Bureau of Public Security and discusses the question with Police Investigator Xiao Huang and says that if they can find out which of the sixteen cars can steer automatically, that will be the one which was bought in Canton.

19. The two split up to carry out the investigation. In the guest registration book at the New Asia Hotel Li Ming-gang sees the name of one of the passengers, a bachelor, Qian Jia-ren, and asks the receptionist if he is in. "Just gone out" is the reply.

20. The receptionist goes to the window and points. "Ah! That's Qian Jia-ren! He's waiting by a taxi." Li Ming-gang takes a look and sees a man dressed in western style just about to get into a taxi.

21. Li Ming-gang hurries down from the hotel and follows Qian Jia-ren by car. He waits until Qian gets out of the taxi and goes into a building and then immediately arranges for the head of the street committee to fetch the governess of the family, Auntie Liu.

22. He asks Auntie Liu to see if the visitor has brought a battery-operated car and if so, to find some way of bringing it out so that he can have a look.

23. Qian Jia-ren has come to see Professor He Jing-xi. They are relatives but have not seen each other for a number of years. Qian takes out a bottle of medicine and says, "My father heard that you still have rheumatism and he asked me to come and see you."

24. Professor He gradually leads Qian Jia-ren into the library, chatting all the while, and asks Auntie Liu to pour some tea. Qian Jia-ren says, "This time I've come back. I want to ask your help with something!" Professor He replies, "No need to be polite with one's own family."

25. Qian Jia-ren walks over to Xiao Cai and sees that she is leafing through a book and soldering some wires. The radio is at one side and is making a crackling noise. He quickly says, "Let me have a look," and expertly gives her a hand with it and quickly repairs it.

26. Professor He asks Qian Jia-ren to stay for dinner and also invites him to move in to stay with the family. Qian politely accepts and says that he will move in the following day. At this moment Auntie Liu leads in Professor He's grandson, Little Ping, who cries out, "Uncle!"

27. Qian Jia-ren asks after Little Ping's mother and father. Professor He replies that they are working on Hainan Island and have not taken Little Ping with them for the moment. Qian Jia-ren praises Little Ping for being so lively and bright and brings out the toy car to give him.

28. Auntie Liu takes Little Ping out with her to buy vegetables, and when they turn the corner of the lane, Li Ming-gang and the head of the street committee come up to meet them. Bending towards Little Ping, Li Ming-gang says, "Young friend, what a beautiful little car you've got there! May I see it?" Auntie Liu tells Little Ping to let Li Ming-gang have a look.

29. Li Ming-gang takes the car, switches it on, and tests it on the ground, not expecting to see it stop without turning automatically at the foot of the wall. Feeling somewhat disappointed, he thanks Auntie Liu and also asks her to continue to keep an eye on Qian Jia-ren.

30. On another street a crowd of children surround Xiao Huang, the investigating officer. They are happily watching the glove puppet on his hand. He says, "Monkey shakes hands with you and asks you to let him play with your toy cars."

31. Xiao Huang tries one after another but all of them stop upon coming into contact with the wall. All he can do is bring the show to an end by saying, "Monkey doesn't like playing with cars. You can all take them away now."

32. At midday Xiao Huang goes to the home of an old factory worker, Lin De-xiang. Lin brings out the toy car which his nephew, Lin Yong-gui, has brought back from Hong Kong. Xiao Huang gives it a try and, as if he has just received a jewel, says, "This is the one! This is the one!"

33. No sooner has Lin De-xiang put the toy car back in its original place than Lin Yong-gui returns. Lin introduces Xiao Huang as a fellow worker from the factory. Xiao Huang takes his leave, saying, "Uncle De, I'm going home to eat. We'll carry on our chat at the factory!"

34. That afternoon Xiao Huang goes to the factory to find Uncle De and to inquire into Lin Yong-gui's past history. Uncle De says, "Before Liberation my elder brother was out of work so he took Yong-gui to Hong Kong to look for a job. Later my brother died; Yong-gui never returned until this very day."

35. Xiao Huang returns to Li Ming-gang to report. Li Ming-gang says, "In several of the spy cases recently smashed by the Bureau, the enemy has been trying to disrupt the public electricity system on the eve of National Day. Lin Yong-gui's uncle works in an electric power station and so we should be extra careful."

36. After his evening meal Uncle De stretches out for a rest, feeling depressed at what Xiao Huang had told him. He hears Yong-gui talking with his wife in the courtyard. She is persuading him not to return to Hong Kong but to find work in Canton. Yong-gui says if his uncle can introduce him to some work, that would be excellent.

37. Unable to contain himself, Uncle De comes out of the room and asks Yong-gui harshly, "What are you thinking of doing?" Yong-gui replies, "As long as I can follow you, Uncle, whatever I do will be all right." Uncle De asks, "What did you do in Hong Kong?" Yong-gui replies, "I worked." Uncle De is furious.

38. Lin Yong-gui stands horror-struck and Uncle De tells him to come inside and then says seriously, "The Lin family from generation to generation has relied on its own hands to make a living; it has never harmed others nor done anything wrong."

39. Uncle De's wife quickly separates them and pushes Uncle De to one side while sending Yong-gui upstairs to sleep.

40. Lin Yong-gui, dismayed, goes upstairs, and Aunt De returns to the room. Seeing that Uncle De is still angry, she asks him, "What on earth is it all about?" Uncle De leads her to sit down and whispers a few sentences into her ear.

41. Lin Yong-gui sits alone in the bedroom upstairs, furiously chain-smoking. He thinks of Uncle De's words, "The Lin family from generation to generation. . . ." but fears that if he confesses he will not be granted a reduced sentence and worries about what will happen to him. He spends a sleepless night.

42. The next morning before Lin gets up, there is the sound of someone ringing the doorbell, followed by the voice of his aunt, "Yong-gui, get up! There's someone looking for you!" In a terrible fright, he dresses as quickly as possible.

43. When he gets downstairs he sees a public security man. It is Li Ming-gang, who looks him straight in the eye and says, "Are you Lin Yong-gui? I've brought something for you. You left it at Shumchun."

44. Li Ming-gang takes a small toy car out of the bag and puts it on the table, saying, "This is yours." Lin Yong-gui says in a scared voice, "No, this is not mine—mine is upstairs." And he quickly goes up to fetch it.

45. Li Ming-gang takes Lin Yong-gui's car and puts them both on the table and tests them and then reminds Lin, "You bought that car in the West Bank Department Store after you had discarded your bag in the station, didn't you?"

46. Lin Yong-gui had still planned to bluff his way out, but faced with such damning evidence and the stern accusing look in the eyes of his uncle and aunt, he can only lower his head and confess.

47. In the Bureau of Public Security, Lin Yong-gui confesses, "The object of my coming back to Canton was to blow up the electricity transforming plant; the time was fixed for seven o'clock on the evening of September thirtieth." Li Ming-gang asks if there are any people involved inside the plant and Lin says there are none.

48. Li Ming-gang asks who they are sending and Lin replies he does not know. Li then asks where the bomb is coming from and Lin replies, "It was planned that I would go to the station on September twenty-eighth where there would be a message on the message board."

49. Li Ming-gang once again explains the policy of the government: to take a serious view of failure to co-operate but to treat leniently those who confess, to reward those who acquit themselves well, and he gives some examples. Lin understands and only then does he confess completely.

50. On the afternoon of September 26 Lin is called to the neighborhood telephone post to receive a call. The caller, using code, tells him to bring Que Da-cheng to the front of the West Bank Department Store between two-forty-five and three o'clock.

51. At the appointed time Li Ming-gang sends Xiao Huang to hide in the department store while he and Lin Yong-gui go to the rest area of the store. He pretends to be playing with a toy while keeping careful watch on passers-by.

52. After a short while, a woman walks in and sits behind Li and begins to arrange her newly bought parcels. Li sees nothing suspicious about her and takes no further notice.

53. A child falls over in the passageway and Li Ming-gang quickly starts forward to pick him up; but he suddenly realizes that this could give him away and sits down again. The woman sitting behind is watching carefully and does not miss any of this.

54. Lin Yong-gui looks at the wall clock and then worriedly says, "It's past the time, what are we going to do?" "Let's wait a bit longer," says Li Ming-gang, and turning his head he sees the woman stand up and go to the mirror, where she re-arranges her hair and calmly walks out.

55. Xiao Huang, who has been watching the woman from his hiding place, goes over to the mirror and has a look in it and finds that it gives a good view of Li Ming-gang and Lin Yong-gui.

56. Xiao Huang immediately trails the suspicious woman and sees her entering a clothing co-operative. Xiao Huang learns from the neighboring police station that her name is Xu Ying. From what they say, he learns that she works fairly well, and as for the rest, they don't know anything about her.

57. Xu Ying returns to her home. Feeling very tired, she smokes a cigarette, looks at her watch, and then bundles up some clothes and sets out again.

58. She slips out the back lane and in a few steps she is at Professor He's house. Outside the back gate she says to Auntie Liu, "I've brought some clothes for Xiao Cai. Has she gone to work?" Auntie Liu replies, "She's in the guest room talking with a visitor. Come in!"

59. Xu Ying goes into the guest room and sees Qian Jia-ren and Xiao Cai working on the radio and says, "Xiao Cai, your clothes are ready." Xiao Cai is delighted and Xu Ying says, "Try them on and if they don't fit, I'll alter them."

60. Xiao Cai takes the clothes and goes upstairs. Xu Ying checks that all is quiet upstairs and Qian Jia-ren checks outside; seeing that there is nobody in sight, they quickly exchange a glance.

61. Xu Ying lowers her voice and says, "I don't think Lin Yong-gui is reliable. The person called Que did not look as if he was taking orders from Lin, but on the contrary it seemed as if Lin was following his instructions." Qian Jia-ren laughs coldly and says, "Let's keep clear of the bastard! We'll look after ourselves!"

62. Xu Ying wants Qian Jia-ren to contact Hong Kong, to tell the courier bringing money not to contact Lin Yong-gui. After a moment's thought, Qian says cunningly, "No, let's have him sent after all! I've thought of a way of getting the money through."

63. Xu Ying also says, "There's something else. Give Lin Yong-gui a telephone call. They're bound to know we have people in Canton—tell him to get out as soon as he can!" Qian Jia-ren says with a shrug, "There's nothing we can do to get him out."

64. Just then, they hear footsteps. Both immediately break away: Qian pretends to be fixing the radio while Xu pretends to be waiting for Xiao Cai. Xu sees that it is Auntie Liu coming in and starts to chat with her.

65. That evening, Qian Jia-ren gives Lin Yong-gui a telephone call. "I had some business this afternoon," he says, "so I could not make the appointment; I'm extremely sorry. A letter has come from Hong Kong telling me to go back. As for Que Da-cheng, let's consider the matter closed. As for the goods you needed, you can pick them up as arranged."

66. After hearing the call, Li Ming-gang busily carries on his preparations. On the twenty-eighth he and Xiao Huang are sitting in the station waiting room, holding a newspaper and keeping a careful watch on the message board.

67. After a long wait, a man carrying a shoulder bag goes up to the message board and after looking right and left, sticks a notice up on the board.

68. As soon as the man has walked off, Li Ming-gang turns to a plain-clothes comrade from the Public Security Bureau and sends him to follow the fellow. Just at this moment Qian Jia-ren appears from another direction; his eyes quickly sweep the message board and he then hurries out of the station.

69. After a while Lin Yong-gui takes down the piece of paper. The message is that the goods are under a seat marked with flour beside the lake in Yue-xiu Park.

70. Li Ming-gang and Lin Yong-gui have arrived in Yue-xiu Park. They find the seat with the flour mark beside the lake and also find a footprint in the sand apparently recently made. Li takes a careful look at it and then photographs it.

71. Kneeling down, Li discovers a bundle under the seat. Opening it he finds a bomb and a time clock. Both he and Lin gasp.

72. Meanwhile the man with the shoulder bag, having finished his mission, hopes to steal back over the border to Hong Kong. Little does he realize that Xiao Huang has been following him day and night, and just as he is walking onto the bridge at the border crossing, Xiao Huang and the border guards arrest him.

73. The fellow makes a full confession in the Bureau of Public Security: his job was only to deliver the bomb, nothing more. When Li Ming-gang produces the parcel which has been under the seat, he takes a close look at it and says that although the wrapping is the same as he had used, the things inside are much smaller; he had put two much bigger parcels there.

74. After the careful questioning is over, Li Ming-gang says to Xiao Huang, "It's all very clear. He had two bombs in the packet, and before we got to the park somebody must have taken one of them and left the other in order to confuse us. The key to the problem is the footprint."

75. Li Ming-gang and a neighborhood policeman have come to the back of Professor He's house. The policeman says, pointing, "This is the He residence—that is Xu Ying's house. Since Qian Jia-ren moved in, we have found that Xu Ying frequently visits using the back entrance."

76. Li Ming-gang asks the policeman what sort of person Professor He is and the policeman replies, "He's been living here a long time. There's never been any trouble." Li asks who is in the family. "There's a niece, Xiao Cai, who works in the electricity transforming station."

77. At the mention of the electricity transforming station, Li Ming-gang's suspicions are alerted and he immediately sets off for the electricity station to find out about Xiao Cai. He sees a girl adjusting the switches and guesses she is Xiao Cai.

78. One of the old workers tells Li Ming-gang, "Xiao Cai is very active in her work and likes to study radio." Li asks if she is on duty on National Day and the old worker replies she is.

79. Li Ming-gang returns to the local police station and has Auntie Liu fetched. He asks her detailed questions about the people in the He family. Auntie Liu says, "This Qian man is very friendly with Xiao Cai; they spend the whole day together working on the radio."

80. As soon as Auntie Liu says this, Li Ming-gang quickly asks, "What kind of shoes does Qian wear?" Auntie Liu thinks awhile and then replies, "Leather shoes. One pair is black with hard soles. The other is yellowish with rubber soles."

81. Back in the Bureau, Li Ming-gang and Xiao Huang agree that Xu Ying is one of the enemy's concealed agents and that her proximity to the He family has been used to get a footing there, to find out through Xiao Cai conditions at the electricity transforming station and then send in Qian Jia-ren.

82. Walking to the window Li Ming-gang sees lanterns and banners being put up in the avenue and gongs and drums being beaten. A propaganda car drives by announcing on its loudspeaker: ". . . Everybody is requested to pay particular attention to the traffic rules to preserve safety on National Day." When he hears the words "preserve safety on National Day," Li Ming-gang feels secretly ill at ease.

83. Since time is so short, Li Ming-gang decides to go directly to Professor He and sound out the situation. Xiao Huang reckons that Professor He and Qian Jia-ren are implicated together and fears that such a course of action will not result in much.

84. Li Ming-gang says, "I believe that although at times the masses of today can be misled, as soon as they understand the past they see what's what, like Lin Yong-gui's uncle, an excellent example." Li and Xiao Huang work out a plan to flush the game from its cover and first think of a method of getting Xiao Cai and Qian Jia-ren out of the house.

85. A short while later, Xiao Cai suddenly receives a call from the electricity transforming station requesting her to arrive early, at exactly six o'clock, for work. Qian Jia-ren quickly invites both her and Professor He to go to a restaurant with him at five o'clock to celebrate National Day.

86. Waiting beside the fruitseller's stall by the He house, Li and Xiao Huang see Qian and Xiao Cai leaving the house. Li then orders Xiao Huang to wait in the neighboring police station while he himself goes into the house.

87. When Professor He sees Li Ming-gang's letter of introduction he supposes Li has come to arrange a job for Qian Jia-ren and delightedly says, "Ah! Jia-ren is pretty skilled, I think he's pretty reliable."

88. On hearing this public security agent asking questions about Qian Jia-ren's activities and his relations with Xiao Cai, Professor He's suspicions are aroused. Li Ming-gang says straight out to him, "Qian Jia-ren is involved in a spy case," and he takes out a photograph of the footprint found by the lake.

89. Li Ming-gang wants Professor He to fetch Qian Jia-ren's shoes and compare them with the photo but Professor He says that it would not be right to go through a guest's belongings when he was out. Li Ming-gang looks at his watch and although anxious, he patiently explains the situation to Professor He.

90. Li Ming-gang continues, "If the enemy, using your protection, destroys the public electricity system this evening, many people will be hurt and it's possible that even your niece will be harmed." The more he hears, the more Professor He realizes the danger and his fighting spirit is awakened.

91. Professor He gets up and walks into Qian Jia-ren's room. He brings out a pair of yellowish shoes and places them in front of Li Ming-gang.

92. The photo tallies exactly with the sole of the shoe: the length is the same and the level of imprint of the patterned heel fits. Professor He's face turns white and he asks Li Ming-gang to check over Qian Jia-ren's room.

93. Li Ming-gang asks Professor He to replace the disarranged things. The Professor, however, finds a plastic tube in the suitcase and asks what it is. Li takes a look and says it is an ordinary plastic tube and tells him to put it back quickly.

94. Li Ming-gang opens the drawers of the dresser and takes out a leather box and asks, "Is this also his?" "Yes, it is a universal meter, he said he was going to give it to Xiao Cai." Just as Li is about to open it they hear the doorbell.

95. Li Ming-gang quickly replaces the universal meter in its original position and says in a low voice, "Professor He, do as I say, quickly." They go back to the library and, just like two old friends, sit opposite each other playing Chinese chess.

96. Qian Jia-ren comes in from the courtyard saying, "Professor He, Xiao Cai has gone off with some of her classmates. I walked around for a bit and then came back!"

97. Li Ming-gang stands up and says hello to Qian Jia-ren, while Professor He introduces him, saying, "This is Professor Li, a colleague of mine." Qian Jia-ren politely nods and says hello. Professor He turns to Li and says, "This gentleman is a relative of mine, Qian Jia-ren."

98. Qian Jia-ren goes up to his room and looks around carefully, while listening surreptitiously to what is going on in the library.

99. Qian Jia-ren is extremely worried and bursts into the library saying, "Professor He, it's almost time. Let's go out and eat."

100. Professor He feels very upset and tries to persuade Li Ming-gang to go with them. Li excuses himself. The cunning Qian Jia-ren immediately senses that something is wrong and so, changing his tune, says, "Let's go another day, then. But how can we let Xiao Cai know?"

101. Qian Jia-ren goes back to his room, takes out the universal meter, and puts it in his brief case. Just as he is about to leave he suddenly catches sight of Li Ming-gang on his way to fetch a glass of water, casting a searching glance into the room. Qian gets a terrific shock and quickly draws back into the room.

102. Li Ming-gang, using the excuse that there is no boiled water left in the thermos flask, asks Professor He to call Auntie Liu to put some on. That's what he says, but he has quickly taken out a note pad and written a message for Auntie Liu to take outside.

103. Auntie Liu finds Xiao Huang by the fruitseller's stall and gives him the message from Li Ming-gang. Xiao Huang sees the brief message, "The bird has flown the cage," and understands.

104. Xu Ying has bought two boat tickets and is waiting for Qian Jia-ren to put the bomb in position before escaping with him. She is just smoking and waiting when suddenly she hears someone knocking at the door and she is startled.

105. Xu Ying opens the door to find the head of the street committee with an ant-control worker. Says the street leader, "Several of the neighbors have found white ants. This comrade wants to investigate the ants' route."

106. The white-ant worker is none other than Xiao Huang in disguise. He taps the walls, looks under the bed. Xu Ying coldly watches and then, suddenly realizing that things are not looking too good, she asks the street committee leader to lock up for her as she has some urgent business to look after. So saying, she turns and leaves.

107. When Li Ming-gang sees that Qian Jia-ren has still not gone out, he says in a loud voice, "Goodness me! I've been playing chess all this while and I've forgotten to give the family a call. I'll go out for a second to give them a ring and then be right back." Just at this moment Xu Ying comes hurrying in looking for Auntie Liu.

108. Xu Ying says in a loud voice directed toward Qian Jia-ren's room, "Just now the street committee came round to my place to search it; they say white ants have been discovered and every house has to be searched. I came to borrow a chemical sprayer. . . ." When she turns and sees Li Ming-gang has returned, she is startled, but Li pretends he hasn't noticed.

109. Qian Jia-ren hears Xu Ying's hidden warning and nearly jumps out of his skin. But seeing that Li Ming-gang has gone out and thinking this is an opportunity not to be missed, he picks up the leather box and walks out of his room.

110. Qian Jia-ren goes into the lavatory, opens the lid of the cistern, and takes out the bomb. He sets the hands of the clock to seven o'clock and hides the bomb in the box under the universal meter.

111. Qian Jia-ren goes to the sitting room to take his leave of Professor He just as Li Ming-gang returns from telephoning. Li stands in the door and, smiling, says, "Mr. Qian, are you going out to take photographs? Take a photo of us, won't you?"

112. Qian Jia-ren walks over, opens the universal meter box and tests it, then quickly puts on the lid as if to say, "You see, there's nothing!" Li Ming-gang smiles and lets him pass.

113. Qian Jia-ren breaks out into a cold sweat and quickly says, "Professor He, Mr. Li, I'm off now." He picks up the box and, trying to appear unhurried, leaves.

114. When Li Ming-gang hears that Qian Jia-ren had gone into the lavatory, he quickly goes up to take a look. As soon as he sees the cistern flooding and a pool of water on the floor below it, he understands where the bomb had been hidden and turns to nod to Professor He.

115. Li Ming-gang says, "I went out just now on purpose to set Qian Jia-ren at rest and at the same time to tell Xiao Huang to guard Xiao Cai. Now everything is very clear. The bomb was hidden in the cistern and without doubt he has used the universal meter box to take it out in. Don't worry, Professor He, we'll destroy their plan in no time."

116. Meanwhile Xiao Cai has been waiting for Qian Jia-ren outside the restaurant, and seeing that it is almost time to go to work she is getting anxious. All of a sudden she catches sight of Qian Jia-ren dashing up. As soon as he sees her he says, "I'm terribly sorry, Professor He had guests at the house and can't come. Let me take you to the transforming station."

117. Qian Jia-ren helps Xiao Cai into the car and they start off. Little does he think that Xiao Huang is in another car following them.

118. Qian Jia-ren gives the universal meter to Xiao Cai, saying considerately, "This is really nothing very special; I've noticed you spend all day working on radios. It really is something you need—please keep it for your own use!" But Xiao Cai is unwilling to accept it.

119. Seeing that Xiao Cai is not going to accept, Qian Jia-ren changes his tactics and says, "Let's say I'm keeping it in your place. You use it and then we'll talk about it again later." Xiao Cai agrees and Qian reaches over and puts the universal meter in her bag.

120. The car arrives at the power station and Qian Jia-ren watches Xiao Cai go in, a cold smile on his face.

121. Going into the switch room and taking out the universal meter, Xiao Cai quite unashamedly runs her hands over it. All of a sudden somebody shouts, "Xiao Cai, someone is looking for you, go to the guard room quickly." Xiao Cai is startled.

122. The comrade in the guard room introduces Li Minggang and then lets Li open the box in front of Xiao Cai. He takes out the universal meter and the bomb and time clock from underneath.

123. When Xiao Cai discovers that she has been used by the enemy, she feels dreadful. Suddenly the telephone rings and Li Ming-gang picks up the receiver. It is Xiao Huang calling to say that Qian Jia-ren is escaping toward the harbor; he requests that Li go down to the wharf to help with the arrest.

124. As soon as Xiao Huang puts down the receiver, he quickly jumps into a car with two policemen and they hurry down to the harbor jetty to find that the ferry has just left.

125. The three take a motorboat and speed off in pursuit of the ferry.

126. When they catch up with the ferry, they search it with the aid of the crew and find Xu Ying and ask her, "What about the other person?" Xu Ying denies all knowledge. Xiao Huang says sternly, "Don't pretend you don't know! Your two boat tickets were bought together."

127. Just as Li Ming-gang arrives at the harbor, he sees Xiao Huang and the two policemen with Xu Ying in custody stepping on to the jetty. Li Ming-gang quickly asks, "What about Qian Jia-ren?" Xiao Huang says, "We searched the whole boat but didn't get him."

128. Li Ming-gang orders the two policemen to take Xu Ying away. Next he and Xiao Huang board the motorboat and speed after the ferry, carefully checking all around.

129. When the motorboat gets to the stern of the ferry, Li Ming-gang notices a small wave to the side of the rudder and just below it a bunch of seaweed.

130. He spreads the seaweed and finds a plastic tube sticking out of the water. He immediately remembers that this is the tube he had seen in Professor He's house and he begins to put two and two together. Reaching forward he pinches the tube shut.

131. Bubbles burst on the surface and Li Ming-gang smiles. Next the bubbles get larger and larger and then, with a gasping noise, a man's head appears. It is Qian Jia-ren.

132. As he comes out of the water, the spy Qian Jia-ren is spitting and gasping for breath. Li Ming-gang orders him into the boat and he climbs in. As soon as he sees Li he realizes the game is up and huddles to one side, shivering.

133. As Li Ming-gang and Xiao Huang victoriously return in the boat, the clock tower on the bank is just striking seven and the whole town is filled with lights and singing. Canton on the eve of National Day presents a joyful and bustling appearance.

LETTERS FROM
THE SOUTH

Size 12.5 x 10 cm

*Story adapted from a Vietnamese original by
    Sha Se, Fu Tuo, Ma Rong, Li Qi-huang*

Adapted by Li Bai-ying

Drawings by Chen Yun-hua and Hu Zu-qing

*Published by the Shanghai People's Art
    Publishing Co., Shanghai, 1965*

Number of copies printed: 282,500

1. It was 1962, and one afternoon, A Xuan, the Party branch secretary of the South Vietnam People's Revolutionary Party in the "strategic hamlet" of Dong Fang, was discussing with Tu Dai Ba, a member of the Party branch committee, A Ha, and others how to organize the revolutionary forces to destroy the strategic hamlet.

2. Suddenly A Ha's mother came rushing in and said angrily, "The enemy have come into the village again! They're forcibly taking the people's goods, forcing them to hand over tax rice."

3. A Xuan and the others hurried into the village and saw the captain of the sentry post by the village gate with several puppet army soldiers, threateningly asking an old villager why he had not handed over his tax.

4. The old man stood his ground and then, staring the captain full in the face, shouted, "So that I can give the grain to the guerrillas, so that they can eat their fill and then wipe you out!"

5. The puppet captain was startled at first and then said, "I'll make an example of you! You're the ringleader!" So saying, he grabbed a pickax and with a shout advanced toward the old man

6. The people were furious and let out a roar. A Xuan shouted, "Fellow villagers, don't be frightened! We must stand firm and fight!" The enemy was scared stiff and scuttled off with his tail between his legs.

7. The puppet captain hurried back to the guard post, ordered extra men to stand sentry duty, and reported to his American chief. Late that night the American "adviser," Kent, led the puppet army in a surprise raid on the village.

8. These robbers arrested people left, right, and center and eventually departed, taking A Xuan, Tu Dai Ba, and twenty others.

9. The villagers were furious as they waited day and night for the return of their arrested dear ones. At dawn on the third day A Ha's elder sister, A Ngoc, was discussing the arrest of her husband, A Xuan, and suggested going to the town to make inquiries.

10. A Ha's mother said, "Your cousin Van An is a teacher in a high school in the town. Why don't you just ask him to go to the police station and make inquiries?" Just as they were talking there suddenly came the sound of someone knocking lightly but urgently.

11. A Ha hurriedly opened the door; it was a moment before she realized that the wild-eyed man covered with wounds who burst in was Tu Dai Ba, who had been arrested three days before.

12. She quickly led Tu Dai Ba into the room, shut the door, and asked him how he had managed to return. Tu Dai Ba replied, "Last night the American robbers and the secret police took us to Lake Lam and tried to force us to tell them who were members of the Vietcong."

13. "Everybody kept their mouths shut. Then they shot five of us. The last to be shot was . . . was Comrade A Xuan. He died heroically shouting the slogan . . ."

14. At this A Ngoc buried her head in her mother's breast. Tu continued, "The enemy got nothing out of us. They threw the comrades' bodies into the lake. As they dragged me back to the town, I jumped into the lake and escaped by swimming."

15. A Ha said angrily, "We must not allow the blood of our martyred comrades to have been shed in vain!" Tu said that that was why he had come back to the village, to strengthen the Party branch and lead the masses to continue the fight.

16. Tu also said to A Ha, "I've already been to the district committee. They've decided that you are to take over as Party branch secretary. They also want me to make contact with the guerrillas to request replacements for the arrested comrades and strengthen us for the fight on the strategic hamlet."

17. Just as Tu Dai Ba was about to leave, they heard a dog bark. A Ha quickly blew out the lantern and gently opened the door to see what was going on outside.

18. Just as she got outside, Han Ngu, who lived next door, dashed up and said breathlessly, "Is Tu with you? Just now my husband came back and he said that the enemy were coming to arrest Tu Dai Ba. Tell him to hide quickly."

19. Han's husband, although he hated the enemy, had been forced to enlist in the puppet army of South Vietnam. A Ha waited until Han had gone and then helped Tu Dai Ba into a hiding place which she carefully covered with leaves and grass.

20. The clucking of the chickens, the barking of the dogs, and the shouting of the captain of the puppet army all mingled together. The searchlight on the guard post cast its ghostly beam round the village as the puppet troops began a house-to-house search.

21. The enemy's search went on half the night, but they found nothing and angrily left the village. A Ha called Tu Dai Ba out from the hiding place and said, "The enemy are searching for you. You'd better not leave the village yet but wait in hiding a few days."

22. Tu Dai Ba anxiously asked, "But who will go to the guerrillas then?" A Ha replied, "I'll go. I know that area. You look after our work in the village while I'm gone, but lie low." Tu Dai Ba saw how trustworthy she was and, after a moment's reflection, agreed.

23. He handed her the letter of introduction from the Party and taught her the password for the guerrillas and then urged her to take care on the way.

24. A Ha memorized the password as she disguised herself in a puppet army uniform and hid the medicine which the villagers had brought back from the town in a shoulder bag before setting off that very night for the guerrillas.

25. The afternoon of the next day, just as she was approaching the area, a man suddenly burst out from the jungle and holding his gun on her, shouted, "Don't move!"

26. A Ha thought he looked like a guerrilla and was about to ask, when he grabbed her shoulder bag and glancing aside said, "Ugh! It's full of poison. You wanted to poison the guerrillas!"

27. He flung the bag into the jungle and taking out some cord, made A Ha turn round and then fastened her wrists, saying as he did so, "It's April twenty-eighth and I've captured another prisoner."

28. A Ha went on, "I'm from the strategic hamlet on urgent business. I must see the leadership of the guerrillas. Who are you?" The old man said, "So you want to ask me the questions first, do you? Well, I'll tell you. . . ."

29. Duong Lao Thanh shouted, "That's enough! Who's your comrade! Get moving and keep your eyes to the front!" So saying, he took her at gun point to the headquarters of the People's Armed Self-Protection Force.

30. When they got to the headquarters, Commander Le had just returned from a victorious surprise attack. Thanh reported to him that he had just captured a woman soldier of the puppet army.

31. Commander Le ordered Duong Lao Thanh to untie A Ha's wrists. She happily cried, "Comrade Commander!" and then started forward to shake his hand, but the two militia guarding her ordered her to keep still.

32. A Ha realized how suspicious she must appear and quickly used the password: "Are there any tigers here, neighbor?" Commander Le answered, "Plenty. Are you afraid?" A Ha used the answer Tu Dai Ba had taught her.

33. Comrade Le stepped forward and grasping her hands in both of his, said with emotion, "Comrade, what's your name?" It was only then that A Ha revealed who she was.

34. A Ha handed him the letter of introduction from the Party and he suggested that she rest a while.

35. Duong Lao Thanh shook her hand and said, "I would never have thought you were A Ha; you've grown so quickly. You're already a young woman. Is your mother well? It's been several years since I last saw her. . . . Please excuse the way I treated you just now."

36. The militia poured some drinking water for A Ha, gave her biscuits, and generally looked after her. A Ha felt very warm toward them but when she thought of the miserable life in the strategic hamlet and the comrades who had been arrested and put in jail she began to cry.

37. She wiped away her tears and then told them of the criminal acts of the enemy in the village. Finally she said, "The people in the strategic hamlet are clenching their fists waiting for the moment when with you they will smash the strategic hamlet and release the imprisoned comrades!"

38. When Duong Lao Thanh and the other militiamen heard of the conditions in the village, they were furious and wanted to go into action then and there to pay off the debt of blood with blood. In one voice they asked Commander Le to give the order.

39. Commander Le told them not to be impatient and then questioned A Ha in detail on the conditions in the village and the strength of the enemy. He then told her, "Comrade A Ha, I'll go immediately and report the situtaion to area headquarters and, depending on their instructions, let you know what the decision is."

40. Commander Le and two militiamen set off for area headquarters while A Ha told the comrades what had happened to the medicine she had brought. Duong Lao Thanh blushed and hurriedly set off to search for the shoulder bag.

41. Just as everyone began to give up hope that he would find it, Duong Lao Thanh reappeared holding up the bag and shouting, "Here's the medicine Comrade A Ha brought for us! Only a bit got lost when I threw it into·the ravine. The comrades in the strategic hamlet don't give the enemy a scrap, but they send us medicine."

42. The more Duong Lao Thanh spoke, the more excited he became and his voice rose as he solemnly handed the medicine to the medical worker, telling her to look after it carefully. Then, turning to the rest of the comrades, he said, "Comrades, this is not medicine—it is the hearts of the people!"

43. Duong Lao Thanh then turned to A Ha and thanked her again. A Ha said, "If the enemy wants something from us, we give them nothing, but when it comes to our own comrades, we give them whatever they need!"

44. That evening Commander Le returned from area headquarters and told A Ha what his instructions were. His eyes flashed and a smile played at the corners of his mouth and he appeared extremely happy.

45. "When you get back," he said to A Ha, "rouse the masses in the strategic hamlet to mount a demonstration in the town. In this way the shocking crimes of the reactionary U.S.-Ngu clique will be exposed and the enemy's attention will be diverted to the town while we smash the strategic hamlet.

46. "In this way we can link up the urban struggle with the rural struggle while combining the political and military struggles to give the enemy a crashing defeat." Then he told A Ha to rest since she would have to set off at dawn the next morning.

47. When A Ha arrived back in the village, she reported the situation to Tu Dai Ba and the other comrades. Everyone was delighted and they decided to separate immediately and go to the strategic hamlets around the town to rouse the masses.

48. A Ha changed into a new dress and went into the town to make contact with the trade union. Just as she was leaving, her mother told her that her cousin Van An had payed a visit while she had been away with the guerrillas. He had been furious at the conditions in the village and wanted to have a talk with A Ha.

49. When she got to town, A Ha found the café where she was to make contact with the trade union and took a seat and ordered a cup of coffee.

50. A newsboy came in selling the evening paper. He was the messenger for the trade union. They exchanged the code word and then A Ha said in a loud voice, "I'll take one!"

51. The newsboy handed her a paper, and as she gave him the money she said in a low voice, "If you see Pham Xuan Ba, tell him A Ha is here."

52. Pham Xuan Ba was the chairman of the underground trade union. After a while he got the message from the newsboy and came up to A Ha and said, "Sister-in-law, I've kept you waiting." A Ha stood up and said, "I've only just arrived. Please sit down."

53. Pham Xuan Ba ordered a cup of coffee and then sat down and said quietly, "Is everything ready?" A Ha replied that they were ready in six villages and that altogether some three thousand people would be taking part. Pham Xuan Ba then told her about the preparations made by the trade union.

54. As soon as Pham Xuan Ba had arranged a date and place for the headquarters for the demonstration, he left. A Ha was about to go also when she saw her cousin Van An coming in, so she called him over.

55. A Ha asked him what he was doing in that sort of place and Van An replied, "When I got back from your house I wrote an article on the actual conditions in the strategic hamlet and sent it to the newspaper offices. Who could have guessed that not only did they not publish it, but they also had me thrown out of my job at the school!"

56. He ordered brandy and drained a glass. A Ha told him with concern in her voice not to get depressed. "Cousin, as Southerners we are in the midst of a struggle against the U.S.-Ngu clique. There is a great deal of work waiting to be done!"

57. A Ha then said in a very serious voice, "The U.S. robbers are supporting the reactionary puppet government, killing and burning wherever they go and turning our beautiful fatherland into a testing ground for 'special warfare.' How can any South Vietnamese just stand by and do nothing!"

58. Van An had long since known that A Ha was no ordinary person and he told her that he was determined to join the struggle against the U.S.-Ngu clique. "If a mass movement develops I hope you will join the ranks."

59. Just then, A Ha noticed that two suspicious characters kept glancing in her direction. Startled, she quickly put on dark glasses, picked up her handbag, and stood up, saying to Van An, "I must go." Van An saw her off.

60. On the sidewalk outside they ran into an old school friend of Van An's, Nguyen Kim. Laughing and chuckling, Nguyen Kim said, pointing to A Ha, "And this is . . ." "A relative of mine," replied Van An.

61. Without waiting to say hello to Nguyen Kim, A Ha hurried off. Nguyen Kim watched her go and then turned to Van An, suggesting that since they had not seen each other for so long they should have a drink together.

62. Seeing how flashy Nguyen Kim looked, Van An asked him what he had been doing since leaving school. Nguyen Kim replied that he had gone with his father to America and had only just got back and was now helping in his father's company. Then he asked Van An what he was doing.

63. Van An told Nguyen Kim how he'd lost his job for having written an article about the strategic hamlet and, growing angry as he spoke, he handed Nguyen Kim a pamphlet that he'd just picked up, saying, "This is the freedom and democracy the Americans are always boasting about!"

64. Nguyen Kim glanced at it and saw that it was a pamphlet exposing the criminal acts of the U.S. devils and the puppet army in South Vietnam. Pretending to be angry, he said, "Terrible! We must expose their inhuman acts to the whole country, to the whole world!"

65. Van An then said that it was best to actively participate in the struggle against the reactionary U.S.-Ngu clique. Nguyen Kim said he had all along wanted to stand and fight together with the people and he hoped Van An would help him. At that point one of the characters who had been watching A Ha earlier came up to Nguyen Kim and began to whisper something to him.

66. Nguyen Kim was in fact the head of special agents in the Ministry of Civil Affairs and a traitor and criminal. When he heard the side-kick's report, he became furious and shouted, "Idiot! She just left—go after her!" But it was too late; A Ha had already disappeared.

67. Van An realized that Nguyen Kim was not to be trusted and, saying good-by, he turned to go. But Nguyen Kim held him back and said, "That relative of yours' was quite something! I would really like to meet her, can you introduce me?"

68. Nguyen Kim grabbed Van An and said, "Not so quick! I need your help badly—take me to that relative of yours!" Van An absolutely refused, so Nguyen Kim said, "Very well, you'll come with me to the Police Bureau!"

69. Van An was taken to the Police Bureau for interrogation. The police commissioner, Ngu Minh Khanh, asked Van An in a conciliatory tone to sit down and said smiling, "We would like to ask your help. Mr. Van An, where does the woman live who had coffee with you just now?"

70. Ngu Minh Khanh chuckled and said, "Mr. Van An, you are a man of intelligence. What's the point of my using threats with you?" Van An stood up and said, "You are wrong. I shall never be a traitor to my people!"

71. Ngu Minh Khanh's face hardened as he glared at Van An and said, "All right! That's fine! Perhaps you want to savor the full range of our American techniques of punishment! Splendid! Take him away and turn the heat on!" Two side-kicks came in and dragged Van An away.

72. The enemy used many different forms of torture on Van An but they could get nothing out of him. Ngu Minh Khanh was thinking of interrogating him again when the telephone rang. No sooner had he picked up the receiver than his face turned pale.

73. A Ha led some three thousand people from the strategic hamlets bursting through the enemy's barricades into the town.

74. They joined up with the workers, students, and monks to form a huge column and then advanced, roaring, "U.S. get out! Down with the U.S.-Ngu clique! Smash the strategic hamlets!"

75. The column surged forward. They demanded that the Police Bureau release those under arrest. Ngu Minh Khanh was in a panic and jumped into a jeep with some soldiers. He tried to frighten the masses into dispersing.

76. The masses were furious and surged forward to surround Ngu Minh Khanh and the police. They snatched those running dogs of the U.S.-Ngu clique out of the jeep and kicked and punched them on the ground. Ngu Minh Khanh was beaten until he was bruised all over and blood trickled from his forehead and his clothes were ripped to pieces.

77. Suddenly a contingent of troops charged forward. The puppet army and the police and spies had joined together. The masses, with clenched fists, joined battle with them. The troops beat up and arrested anyone they could lay hands on, including A Ha.

78. Ngu Minh Khanh had scuttled back to the Police Bureau and had changed his clothes. A girl secretary came in and announced that Special Agent Nguyen Kim had sent someone around with a woman criminal who had been captured during the demonstration and that it was more than possible that she was the leader.

79. A policeman brought in A Ha, and Ngu Minh Khanh stepped forward with a smile to greet her, rubbing his hands together. "Please take a seat." A Ha glared at him. "I don't need your courtesies. If you have anything to say, say it now."

80. Ngu Minh Khanh asked her her name and then stared at her, lost in thought. Suddenly he seemed to have remembered something and said, "Young lady, you've changed your name, haven't you? Weren't you one of the leaders of the strike at the textile mill several years back?"

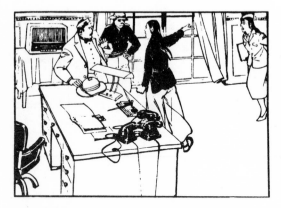

81. A Ha drew herself up to her full height and then accused the commissioner. "Why did you murder our fellow countrymen on the banks of Lake Lam?" Ngu Minh Khanh was about to deny all knowledge when the sound of shouting came in from outside and the secretary came bursting into the room.

82. The demonstrators had braved the tear gas and water cannon of the troops, broken down the barricades, and were now coming in the direction of the Police Bureau. Ngu Minh Khanh frowned as he heard this news and began to mop his brow.

83. He took out a checkbook and held it out to A Ha. "All you have to do is to say a few words to the demonstrators. Tell them that the affair at Lake Lam was a rumor started by some criminals, and tell them to disperse immediately. I can give you a very large dollar reward so that you and your mother can spend the rest of your lives in comfort."

84. Ngu Minh Khanh put the checkbook down and said, "You'll regret this, A Ha! Your relative Mr. Van An should be an example for you. He's already had a taste of our American instruments of torture." A Ha started, for this was the first she had heard of Van An's arrest.

85. By this time the thunderous slogans of the demonstrators could be heard outside and Ngu Minh Khanh was in a tremendous panic. He tried to persuade A Ha to talk to them and this time she agreed. Beside himself with joy, Ngu Minh Khanh quickly grasped the microphone and began shouting into it.

86. Nodding to A Ha, he said, "Go ahead," and A Ha then spoke with all her force into the microphone. "Fellow countrymen! Who was it who organized the affair at Lake Lam? Who was it who murdered our martyrs?"

87. A Ha took no notice of Ngu Minh Khanh who was shouting at her but continued, "If they don't release our imprisoned comrades, punish those responsible for the Lake Lam killings, and abolish the strategic hamlet, we shall not release the troops! We shall drive out the American devils and smash the puppet government!"

88. When they heard A Ha, the demonstrators responded with one voice. Their slogans came thundering out with irrepressible force.

89. Ngu Minh Khanh was jumping up and down with fury and shouted at the police to drag A Ha away.

90. Suddenly the American "adviser" Kent and the head of the secret agents, Nguyen Kim, came dashing in, all out of breath. Kent was furious. "What sort of police chief are you! You can't even manage an unarmed crowd of peasants. I had to slip around the back streets and use the special underground tunnel to get in here!"

91. Ngu Minh Khanh was just giving the order when his secretary came in to report, "The demonstrators have demanded the release of A Ha. They will charge the building if she is not released." Kent immediately said, "I'll take the prisoner with me, she's not safe here!"

92. Stones and bottles began coming through the windows and the roar of the crowd grew closer. Kent, Nguyen Kim, and Ngu Minh Khanh took A Ha and Van An with them and escaped by an underground tunnel.

93. Back in the village, Tu Dai Ba had been organizing the plans for smashing the strategic hamlet, defeating the enemy, and rescuing the imprisoned comrades. That evening he called a meeting of all leaders of small group forces in the village and divided the task among them.

94. "As soon as you hear the sound of the clapper board your group should cut the enemy's telephone wires and then join the guerrillas to attack and enter the guard building." After receiving their instructions, the leaders of the small groups each went to make their preparations. A Ha's mother was just asking to be given a task when Han Ngu came running in.

95. Han Ngu said, "My husband has just come back and says the enemy are taking some prisoners on board the "Liberty." They are weighing anchor early tomorrow to go to the prison on Kon Son Island." Tu Dai Ba said, "Whatever happens, we must release our revolutionary comrades."

96. When A Ha's mother heard this, she glanced at Tu Dai Ba, wondering what he could do. Tu Dai Ba said, "Don't worry, Grandma. Go to the entrance of the village and stand guard. If anything happens, come and report."

97. A Ha's mother went to the entrance of the village; it was windy and dark but among the shadows she saw someone dressed as a policeman coming into the village. She was about to go back and report, but the policeman came toward her and called softly, "Mother of A Ha, it's Duong Lao Thanh!" A Ha's mother paused a second and then turned happily to greet him.

98. The two old comrades-in-arms were delighted to have met each other so unexpectedly. Duong Lao Thanh said with a smile, "I've come from the guerrillas to see Tu Dai Ba and explain that in order to save A Ha and the other prisoners, headquarters has decided to advance the time of attack." A Ha's mother quickly led him into the village.

99. Duong Lao Thanh explained to Tu Dai Ba that the guerrilla detachment was already lying in wait outside the village. Headquarters wanted them to capture the captain of the puppet army headquarters with cunning before beginning the attack, for if the puppet army was without their leader, the fight would be quickly decided and they would be able to save time.

100. While Tu Dai Ba was thinking, A Ha's mother thought of a way of capturing the captain by getting him to come to the village alone. The other two both agreed when she had finished outlining the plan.

101. Tu Dai Ba struck his chest and guaranteed to carry out this task and urged Duong Lao Thanh to return to headquarters and report. Duong Lao Thanh replied that the leadership wanted him to stay in the village until the captain had been captured, at which point they could sound the clapper board and the attack would begin.

102. Duong Lao Thanh and Tu Dai Ba left A Ha's mother to begin the plan to capture the captain. She extinguished the lantern outside the house and then sat in front of the door with her daughter A Ngoc, deliberately waiting for the puppet policemen to come along.

103. After a while, the neighboring lanterns were all extinguished. The strategic hamlet policeman on his rounds of the village noticed this and came over to inquire, "Why don't you light your lantern?" A Ha's mother said, "We haven't got enough money to buy the oil!" The policeman asked suspiciously, "Then why are you sitting at your doorway?" A Ngoc replied, "I felt ill at ease and couldn't sleep."

104. "Rule 13 of the village regulations states," said the policeman, "the fine for not keeping a lighted lantern outside all night is fifty piaster. Fork out!" A Ha's mother said, "We have no money! You've taken it all." The policeman was furious.

105. The policeman shouted, "O.K., O.K., you've called the captain a dog, I'm going to report straightaway!" "Go and report! I said it: dog captain! dog captain!" A Ha's mother went on shouting and cursing the captain. The policeman was furious and rushed off to report.

106. In a short while the policeman came back with the puppet captain, shaking with rage. The policeman pointed at A Ha's mother. "It was she who was insulting you!" The puppet captain glared at her and shouted, "There's a government rule that if someone doesn't light a lantern, they are secretly helping the guerrillas and they will be seriously punished. Didn't you know that?"

107. The puppet captain ordered the policeman to search them and find the fifty piaster for the fine, holding out his hand and saying, "Old woman, let's have the money!" A Ha's mother said in a loud voice, "I haven't a single piaster!"

108. The puppet captain chuckled and glancing at A Ngoc said, "No money? Your daughter's hair is worth a lot. The U.S. company buys young girls' hair for a high price. Cut it!" When A Ngoc heard this, she sprang forward and began cursing the captain.

109. The puppet captain was furious at this, drew his pistol and aimed at A Ngoc. At this, Duong Lao Thanh and a small attack group burst out from where they had been hiding and Duong Lao Thanh smashed the pistol from the captain's hand.

110. One of the young villagers drove his bamboo spear deep into the puppet captain's back. Two of the puppet soldiers were so frightened they surrendered on the spot.

111. They locked the captain and his men in the room and put someone in to guard them. Then Tu Dai Ba beat the bamboo clapper as loud as he could. "Tock . . . Tock . . . Tock . . ." Following the signal, two red rockets appeared in the sky outside the village.

112. Next the sound of heavy gunfire could be heard coming from the entrance to the village. Duong Lao Thanh and Tu Dai Ba led the attack groups to join up with the guerrillas to take the four guard posts and the puppet army headquarters.

113. Under the fierce charges of the villagers and the guerrillas, the bandit troops melted away like ice on a hot stove; some were killed, some ran away, and others surrendered.

114. After the battle had been won, everybody lit brands and set fire to the bamboo palisade and the guard posts of the strategic hamlet, and the flames lit up the night sky.

115. Six strategic hamlets were smashed. Commander Le quickly assembled his forces and, leading an attack group from the village together with A Ha's mother, A Ngoc, and the others, hurried toward the anchorage in the bay to release A Ha and the other captured comrades.

116. Meanwhile Kent had personally brought A Ha and the others on board the destroyer "Liberty." Kent was now drinking in the dining cabin, waiting for dawn when they could start for the island prison. Suddenly Nguyen Kim rushed in saying, "Major, there's an urgent cable from Saigon!"

117. Kent glanced at it. It was from the commander of the U.S. bandits in Saigon, and it ordered Kent to get a list of members of the underground organization of the Vietcong. "Bring A Ha here," he said without looking up.

118. When she was brought in, Kent pretended to be friendly and said to her, "How beautiful the sea looks at night! What do you feel?" A Ha replied furiously, "My motherland's bay is beautiful, but since you monsters are trampling on my country, I only feel a sense of shame!"

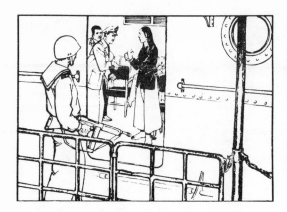

119. Kent pretended to be concerned and said her mother must be longing for her return. A Ha was not in the least bit perturbed but said calmly, "My mother is awaiting the return of a daughter who is of some use to the people, not for a daughter who had surrendered to the enemy and become a traitor to try and save her skin!"

120. Kent removed the shackles on her ankles and wrists saying, "Young lady, I'm an individualist and I'm also a practicing Christian and I'm deeply concerned for the happiness of others, so I've decided to let you live . . ."

121. Kent poured out a glass of champagne and held it out to A Ha, shamelessly saying as he did so, "If you want to help us even more and give us the names of the Vietcong leadership in the town, I can send you to America to study, give you a medal and also a reward . . ."

122. A Ha glared at him and then, "Pow!" she smashed the glass out of his hand and, grinding her teeth, cursed him. "You filthy bandit! You think you can get me to betray my country, sell out my comrades? I'm willing to die standing—I'll never come crying for my life!"

123. Nguyen Kim stepped forward to save his boss from embarrassment and stop A Ha from saying any more. But A Ha pointed straight at him and cursed him to his face. "You stinking traitor, running dog of U.S. imperialism! Helping the enemy to murder your own people, huh! How can you have the nerve to say anything to me?"

124. Nguyen Kim was furious and ashamed at the same time and drew his pistol to shoot A Ha. Kent stopped him and said to A Ha, "Young lady, there is nothing shameful about being on good terms with America. It is a form of friendship and nothing more!"

125. A Ha was even more furious when she heard Kent use the word "friendship" and said accusingly, "Friendship? I ask you! You use napalm bombs to destroy our forests and our rice paddies."

126. "Your airplanes, warships, and tanks spread destruction throughout the motherland, making mothers lose their children, turning young women into widows and children into orphans. Is that your friendship toward the people of South Vietnam, toward the people of Asia?"

127. Kent said, "Young lady, this is really too uncivilized!" A Ha shouted, "It is you who are uncivilized! It is not only in Vietnam that you burn, kill, and pillage, but you set up military bases everywhere, trying to rule the whole world . . ."

128. "Millions upon millions of those who had been enslaved have taken up arms and a new dawn is spreading from the East! Our motherland will be unified. Your bloody crimes will be repaid in blood, you filthy swine! Your days are numbered!" By this time Kent was blushing scarlet and he drew his pistol and fired at A Ha.

129. A Ha staggered back and then, raising her clenched fist, cried, "Long live the unification of the motherland! Long live Uncle Ho!"

130. Just then an American devil came rushing along to report that the guerrillas had appeared on the shore. Kent shouted, "What? Tell the captain to get under way immediately!"

131. Just as Kent and Nguyen Kim were hoping to save their skins, they heard a barrage of gunfire from the shore. At the same time, hand grenades began exploding on the deck as Commander Le led Duong Lao Thanh and the others charging on board the ship.

132. Nguyen Kim began firing but was shot by Duong Lao Thanh. Kent was trying to jump overboard to save himself but Tu Dai Ba dashed forward, grabbed him, and took him prisoner.

133. The battle was over. Han opened the hold and freed the imprisoned comrades. A Ha's mother and A Ngoc found A Ha and helped her up. She had been wounded in the shoulder but it was not a serious wound.

134. The dawn light appeared in the east; it was already day. A Ha said joyously, "Let's quickly write and tell our compatriots in the north, tell Uncle Ho, tell the people of the world, tell them: we are fighting!"

雷　　　锋

LEI FENG

Size 12.5 x 10 cm

*Original film version by Ding Hong, Lu Zhu-guo,
    Cui Jia-jun, and Feng Yi-fu*

Adapted by Wen Piao

Published by China Film Publishers, Peking, 1965

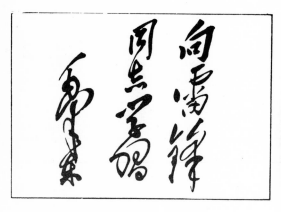

1. **Learn from Lei Feng**
    Mao Ze-dong

Our great leader Chairman Mao has written this inscription calling upon everybody to learn from Lei Feng. We should follow the Party and Chairman Mao's instructions and learn from Lei Feng. We should give our whole bodies and minds to the task of proletarian revolution and be rustless screws in the socialist revolution and in socialist construction.

2. The story of the film **Lei Feng** begins from the time when Lei Feng entered a certain company of the transport corps. Early one morning, having finished a job, Lei Feng drove his truck back to the post.

3. At the post truck pool he backed up into his own place.

4. Just at this moment, a soldier, Wang Da-li, who was in the same squad as Lei Feng, was repairing his truck. He heard a truck backing up, turned around, saw it was Lei Feng, and immediately ran over.

5. Happily he ran up to Lei Feng's truck and seeing that Lei Feng was doing some repairs underneath, knelt down and said, "Lei Feng, you've only just come back and yet you are doing repairs, aren't you tired? Wouldn't it be just as good to do it tomorrow?"

6. As soon as he heard Wang Da-li's voice, Lei Feng sat up and said, "Wang Da-li, how are you? It's a screw which has come loose. I m just tightening it up. There'll be enough to do tomorrow!"

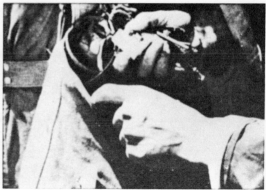

7. As soon as Lei Feng had tightened up the screw, he left the truck and put on his knapsack, ready to go back to the dormitory. Seeing that the knapsack was very full, Wang Da-li said with a smile, "Have you got something tasty in there? Let's all of us have a bite!" Lei Feng laughed and said, "You'd have some trouble biting this!" Wang Da-li stretched out his hand and looked inside the knapsack.

8. What Wang Da-li brought out was definitely inedible: nails, pieces of iron, and so on. These were in fact pieces of scrap which Lei Feng had collected, as he often did, so that when something went wrong with the truck he could use spares from his collection to save state property. However, Wang Da-li, who still had a certain amount of selfish outlook, did not understand.

9. At this moment Wu Kui came up and warmly shook Lei Feng's hand and said, "Oh, you're back. Let's hurry into the dormitory to wash, and since today is Sunday, let's all three go to the park and take some photographs." Wu Kui as a rule liked spending money, and in order to help him develop a sense of austerity and good habits, Lei Feng said, "You said yourself you didn't want to waste any money this month."

10. But Wu Kui took out several notes and said, "My mother has sent me ten **yuan**." Lei Feng said unhappily, "Wu Kui, how can you ask your family for money? Have you already forgotten what I said to you before?" Embarrassed, Wu Kui put the money back into his pocket.

11. Lei Feng, Wang Da-li, and Wu Kui, after having break-fast, went to the park. The Young Pioneers from the Wan Hua Street primary school were having their Pioneers' Day. They were singing and dancing in groups and in circles and having a very lively time. Lei Feng and the others stopped to watch the scene.

12. When the Young Pioneers saw Lei Feng and the others they immediately cried out happily, "The uncles from the Peoples Liberation Army have come." One of them, called Zhou Da-qing, and a young girl quickly came forward to invite the soldiers to join in the play. Lei Feng gently said, "Children, you play; we'll watch you!"

13. The teacher accompanying the Young Pioneers, Teacher Li, came over and said warmly, "The children all very much want the comrades from the Peoples Liberation Army to come and play with them. Don't be polite! Come and join them!"

14. Wang Da-li realized that they would not be able to refuse any longer, so he quickly pointed to Lei Feng and said to Teacher Li, "He can—he's the head of our cultural group. He can dance, sing, or tell stories. He's very good at it!"

15. Hearing this the Young Pioneers took hold of Lei Feng and led him off.

16. Lei Feng always especially liked these blossoms of the fatherland. Although he could not dance, he started to play with the children and felt extremely happy. He skipped and sang along with them.

17. After playing for a while they all went to a pavilion to rest. The children now came out with a new request. "Will the uncle from the P.L.A. tell us a story?" Lei Feng replied, "I've never fought in a war. I couldn't give you a Huang Ji-guang style story!"

18. Zhou Da-qing naïvely said, "Uncle, I don't believe you've never fought." Lei Feng explained again, "Really, I haven't fought in a war." Zhou Da-qing was very observant and said, "I don't believe it, I don't believe it. If you've never fought in a war, then what are those scars on your hand?"

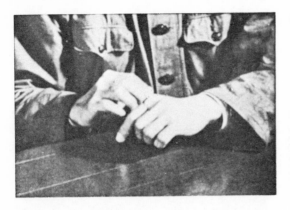

19. Following Zhou Da-qing's question, everybody stared down at Lei Feng's left hand where they saw three scars cut across the back of his hand and fingers. These were the hatred cut into Lei Feng by the old society. The bitterness and hardships of his childhood life now irrepressibly came welling up within his heart scene by scene.

20. Lei Feng slowly said, "This is what is left over from my childhood. My village was in Hunan. I had a father, mother, and elder and younger brother, but none of them lived to see the Liberation."

21. "My father was killed by the Japanese devils. My elder brother died working. My younger brother died of starvation in my mother's arms and my mother died more terribly; following the cruel treatment by the son of the landlord, she took her own life by hanging herself. Our house was a ruined straw hut with battered walls through which the wind whistled. In the winter I would sit shivering, huddled at the foot of one of the walls . . ."

22. "One day as the bitter wind whistled and the snow came drifting into the room like feathers, I was both starving and freezing, and I could only pick up a firewood knife and, with the piece of rope that my mother had used to hang herself, plunge out and brave the bitter cold and search for firewood in the forest . . ."

23. "Just as I was carrying back a bundle of firewood and passing the landlord's doorway, I met the wife of the landlord. She said that the mountainside belonged to her family and therefore the firewood that I had cut belonged to them and she tried to force me to bring it into her house . . ."

24. "I refused, and like a hungry wolf she grabbed me and snatched the firewood away and knocked me onto the snowy ground . . ."

25. "The landlord's wife had also knocked my knife out of my hand, and just as I was stretching out to pick it up, she had already grabbed hold of it and, full of hatred, she slashed me three times with the blade . . ." ·

26. "I fainted and the blood mingled with the snow which was around my hand, frozen stiff like a block of wood . . ."

27. "In 1949 my village was liberated and the Party and Chairman Mao set me free from the depths of misery. In the great warm family of the Revolution I obtained the opportunity to study and joined the Young Pioneers. The Party brought me up like a mother. . . ."

28. When the Young Pioneers heard Lei Feng's account of what had happened to his family before the Liberation, they were deeply moved and class hatred filled their hearts. Teacher Li said to Lei Feng, "Comrade, you spoke so well, we're extremely grateful to you; you have given us an excellent class lesson."

29. That evening the soldiers were standing around the squad room, listening to an important broadcast. "With the support of American imperialism, the bandit gang of Chiang Kai-shek is preparing to enter into a large-scale militaristic adventure and attempting to launch a land and naval attack on the Mainland. . . . If the Chiang gang dares to undertake such an adventure, it will be completely and absolutely wiped out wherever it lands."

30. After the soldiers heard this, they were filled with rage and some said, "Chiang Kai-shek, the traitor, is he still thinking of coming back?" While others said, "He's thinking of coming back to get killed." Lei Feng said firmly, "Come on, let's go and ask the commander to go on active duty!" They were just about to go into the company room when the secretary said to them, "The commander has gone to the Youth League to attend a meeting."

31. At this the soldiers returned to their dormitories. But Lei Feng, after hearing the broadcast, felt the hatred of the class enemy burst out inside his heart and try as he might he could not drive it away. He asked Wu Kui to go back and excuse him while he stood alone outside the commander's office waiting for him to come back. . . . Even after the lamps were extinguished he still did not walk away.

32. Suddenly the warm inquiring voice of the political instructor asked Lei Feng, "What are you doing standing there alone?" Lei Feng turned around and joyously cried, "At last you've come back! What has the regimental command decided about my request?" The instructor said nothing and Lei Feng anxiously enquired, "Did you not put forward my request for an active posting to the regimental command?"

33. The political instructor replied, "We have our duty to do here. What more do you wish to request?" Lei Feng felt dissatisfied by this reply and still unable to control himself. He burst out, "Then I'm going to go to the political commissar and if he doesn't pass it then I shall go further to Shenyang, and if they don't pass it, well, then I'll go to Peking." So saying he turned to go, when the instructor called him back.

34. The instructor told him what a temper he had and Lei Feng replied, "Instructor, you don't understand. I have this bitterness left from the past. . . ." "Lei Feng, that you have not forgotten your class bitterness and that you wish to go fight are all fine things. But you will never achieve your aim by getting overemotional."

35. The instructor, in order to help Lei Feng overcome his problems, invited him into his room where he took out a copy of Chairman Mao's works and prepared to search out an answer in them. The instructor knew that Lei Feng had read the article "Serve the People" more than once, but he purposely asked him if he had read it.

36. Lei Feng did not realize the instructor was asking this on purpose and said, somewhat bewildered, "But, Instructor, it was you yourself who read through this article with us three times already." The instructor replied with a smile, "Oh really? Well, you see, a teacher like myself also has problems."

37. The instructor continued, "All right, I'll test you," and then asked, "Who did Chairman Mao write this article for?" Lei Feng stood up and replied, "For Zhang Si-de." The instructor asked again, "Who was he?" Lei Feng replied, "He was a soldier in the guard of the Central Committee."

38. The instructor asked Lei Feng to sit down and continued his questioning. "How did he sacrifice his life? Was it like Huang Ji-guang, rushing forward to block the enemy's guns? Or was it like Dong Cun-rui, blowing up an enemy gun emplacement?" Lei Feng replied, "No, it was not. He was a charcoal maker in Northern Shensi and his charcoal furnace fell in, killing him." The instructor asked him again, "Well then, why did Chairman Mao say his death was so important?"

39. Lei Feng replied, "Because he sacrificed his life for the people." The instructor said, "That's a good answer. It seems to me that you have read and understood this article very well, but some people don't agree with Chairman Mao. They think that only those like Huang Ji-guang and Dong Cun-rui, who came forward at the battlefront, can be considered real heroes."

40. The instructor continued, "If it is necessary for the good of the people to go out and do the kind of work that Zhang Si-de did, then that type of person gets all upset and he appears to think that he has received a divine injustice. Lei Feng, do you think that way of looking at things is going to lead to serving the people with all one's heart and all one's mind?" When Lei Feng heard this question, he immediately understood what the instructor was getting at.

41. This clear and straightforward advice from the instructor helped Lei Feng resolve his problems of outlook, and he stood up quickly and said, "Instructor, I understand. If the Party and the people require me to go back and do the work of Huan Ji-guang, then I will go and block up the enemy's guns; if they want me to do the work of Zhang Si-de, then I will go and make charcoal. No matter what my role in society, I will fulfill it with all my strength and serve the people in every possible way."

42. Lei Feng continued, "Instructor, never in my life will I forget your criticism." The instructor then placed his hand on Lei Feng's shoulder and said, "Comrade Lei Feng, I was also criticizing myself, for just now I put forward a request for war-posting at the regimental meeting and the chairman of the political committee criticized me strongly. This shows that both of us are fundamentally the same. Neither of us have studied very well and both of us will have to study much better from now on."

43. The instructor took out the four volumes of the **Selected Works of Mao Ze-dong** from a drawer in his desk and said to Lei Feng, "These were given to me as a prize by my superior and now I want to give them to you. I hope that you will study the thought of Chairman Mao as hard as you can."

44. As Lei Feng took these most precious and greatest weapons of revolution, he said to the instructor, "I wish to repay your kindness and advice in my actual behavior."

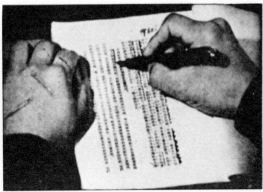

45. From this time on Lei Feng studied the works of Chairman Mao much more actively. On the front of the **Selected Works** he wrote four promises to direct his own conduct:

    Study the works of Chairman Mao every day.
    Do as the Chairman says.
    Follow his instructions in whatever you do.
    Be a good soldier of Chairman Mao's.

46. In every chapter that he read he underlined the important passages and outstanding phrases and he wrote in his diary what he had learned from his studies. He memorized the words of Chairman Mao in his heart.

47. Wherever he went, Lei Feng always read the works of Chairman Mao and during his work, if an opportunity arose, he would take out a copy of the Chairman's works and his diary. Thus he would never allow a precious moment to pass unused.

48. The more he studied the works of Chairman Mao, the more his outlook on life developed, his mind broadened, his political stand grew firm, and his ideals were heightened. If a day passed without being able to study, he felt as if something was missing and he became uneasy.

49. After a great deal of hard study he came to understand how to be a man and what to live for. He derived boundless strength from Chairman Mao's works and in his diary he wrote promises and commitments to encourage himself: "The function of a man in the Revolution is like a screw in a machine. I want to be a rustless revolutionary screw for the rest of my life . . ."

50. Not only did Lei Feng himself study the works of Chairman Mao but he also helped his comrades to study them. He would say to them, "As far as I am concerned, the works of Chairman Mao are like staple crops, like weapons, like a steering wheel. Without crops a man cannot live. It is impossible to make war without weapons and it is impossible to steer a truck without a steering wheel. In the same way, to make Revolution without the works of Chairman Mao is also impossible."

51. One day Lei Feng and Wang Da-li were sent out on a mission with their trucks. Lei Feng and his co-driver Da Cu were in front and Wang Da-li and his co-driver were following behind.

52. Half way there, Wang Da-li began to behave in a liberalist way and drove his truck off the road and encouraged Wu Kui to try to drive. Wu Kui said, "The road is too difficult for me," but Wang Da-li said, "Idiot, why not practice? You have learned to be a soldier, but when you are demobilized you might as well return to your commune with a useful skill." So saying, he brought the truck to a rapid stop and put Wu Kui behind the wheel.

53. Wu Kui was encouraged by Wang Da-li and began to drive backward and forward and around and around on the grass beside the road. Suddenly the truck ran toward a water-filled hole; Wu Kui panicked at the wheel and the truck went into the hole. Both tried to get it out but couldn't manage.

54. Fortunately Lei Feng found them and came in his truck with Da Cu to push them out. When Lei Feng heard how the truck got into the hole he was extremely angry that Wang Da-li should have used public gas and public property for private practice, and he criticized them very strongly.

55. Wang Da-li knew that he had done wrong and said to Lei Feng, "I would like to make a self-criticism about this matter. Don't you report to the instructor; being criticized myself is of no consequence, but I'm afraid that it may spoil our chances of becoming a Four-Good squad!" "Good," said Lei Feng seriously. "I shall not report to the superiors; you can report to them yourself."

56. Following Lei Feng's stern admonishment, Wang Da-li went to the instructor to tell him what he had done. The instructor said, "That you have been able to come and report to me of your own accord and tell me what you did wrong and to criticize your own outlook is very good. But your political consciousness is not high enough. We cultivate our skills in order to raise our fighting strength and fulfill our task of protecting the fatherland. It is not right for individualistic considerations to come into this."

57. The instructor then continued. "Chairman Mao teaches us that we should serve the people with all our hearts and with all our minds; we must not half serve the people and half serve our own interests!" Wang Da-li said, abashed, "Instructor, I was wrong!" Finally the instructor encouraged him to study hard the works of Chairman Mao.

58. From that time on, Wang Da-li's study of Chairman Mao's works became keener. When he came across difficulties Lei Feng enthusiastically helped him and told him that he should fortify his mind with the thoughts of Chairman Mao and put his studies into practice.

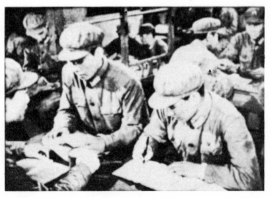

59. As part of the squad's plan to become a Four-Good squad, on Sunday they started a study session and Wang Da-li found in his knapsack an extra copy of the works of Chairman Mao and a new diary. He quickly asked who had mistakenly put them into his knapsack. Wu Kui said, "It was Lei Feng who bought them for you in order to help you study hard and improve your political outlook."

60. Wu Kui also told him that Lei Feng had bought the same for the whole squad but that he had bought an extra diary for Wang Da-li. Wang Da-li immediately remembered how he did not as a rule like keeping a diary. He also felt moved and abashed knowing how careful Lei Feng was not to waste money and yet had bought everybody books. Then without a word he settled down to his studies.

61. Just then they heard Da Cu shout, "Stand up!" It was the instructor who had come in. He asked, "How is it that you are not outside getting some exercise on a Sunday?" Da Cu said, "Sir, this is part of our squad's plan for the Four-Goods. We want to study an extra hour on Sundays." The instructor smilingly said, "But you have already studied two hours today."

62. After the instructor told everyone to sit down again, he took out some money and gave it to Wu Kui, saying, "Wu Kui, your family has sent you more money." Wu Kui took the notes and said, "Ugh, only five **yuan** this time." The instructor criticized him: "Is that not enough for you? You are always asking for money from your family but P.L.A. soldiers should get used to a style of hardship and simple living!"

63. The instructor now walked over to Lei Feng and said with concern, "Haven't you got a cold?" Lei Feng replied, "It's nothing much—just a minor ailment." The instructor said, "Many serious illnesses start in a small way. Hurry up and go to sick bay and have them examine you."

64. Lei Feng acquiesced and then quickly finished his study and said in a loud voice, "Is there anything I can fetch for anybody?" Wu Kui handed him his money and asked him to put it into the bank and Wang Da-li asked him to post a letter. Lei Feng received their commissions and then excused himself to the instructor and went out.

65. Just as Lei Feng went down the road, suddenly from a neighboring work site came the noise of a loudspeaker saying, "Comrades, attention! Very soon there won't be enough bricks at the building site and all building will have to be brought to a halt for lack of bricks." When Lei Feng heard this he forgot his illness and rushed forward to the building site.

66. He went up to a tall worker and said, "Comrade, you've had enough. Take a rest for a while and I'll take over. I want to try and sweat out my cold." The tall worker immediately said, "No. If you take my barrow, I won't be able to finish my own task. If you really want to push one, go and fetch one from the equipment depot."

67. Lei Feng took off his army jacket and quickly ran over to the depot and asked for a barrow from the old man in charge of lending them out. The old man was busy with some accounts and said that the barrows could not be lent off the building site. When he saw that Lei Feng was not going to go away and that he was very small, he pretended to be angry and said, "Where is your family, child? You really are naughty. Hurry up and go away and play."

68. Lei Feng laughed and handed in his army jacket through the window and said with determination, "Old man, please do as I say and take this as a receipt." The old man had not realized that he was a P.L.A. man and said happily, "Oh, it's a P.L.A. man! Yes, of course you can, of course you can," and then lent out a barrow to Lei Feng.

69. Lei Feng rushed the barrow over to the pile of bricks and one of the workmen said, "Great! You really did go and get one," and the tall workman said, "So you do want to work after all." Lei Feng said excitedly, "And I want to challenge you to a race!"

70. The tall workman said, "With that challenge, I'll take you on with a double load!" At that he pushed his heavily loaded cart forward as fast as he could. Lei Feng fell behind at first but gradually caught up and was just about to overtake him when from all over the building site people cheered them on, shouting, "Come on, come on!"

71. Lei Feng flashed by the tall workman and when everybody saw how hard he was working, they all followed suit, loading their barrows as full as they could and going hard at it. A sort of unofficial race got started.

72. The building was in fact an extension for the Wan Hua Street primary school. Teacher Li was working as broadcaster for the building site on that particular day. When she heard that there was a P.L.A. comrade who had come to do voluntary labor, she quickly came over and asked the tall workman where he was. He replied, "He's rushed ahead of me—he's really good, and he's ill too!"

73. Teacher Li caught up with Lei Feng and recognized him as the soldier who had told the story to the children in the park the other day. She shook hands with him and asked after his health and said, "Last time we met I didn't get your name. Could you tell me now, and also give me your squad number?" Lei Feng refused and quickly said, "Oh dear, I'm falling behind," and rushed off with his barrow.

74. Teacher Li ran after him and said, "Comrade from the P.L.A., please tell me why you have come to take part in voluntary labor?" All she caught was the distant answer from Lei Feng, "In order to add one more brick to socialist construction!"

75. Teacher Li was deeply impressed by Lei Feng's lofty spirit and returned to the broadcasting post to broadcast over the loudspeakers, "Comrades, here is an important notice. At this moment there is a P.L.A. comrade who has given up his free day and, although he is ill, has come to take part in voluntary labor. Particularly noteworthy is the fact that he refuses to give his name or squad number. Let's all learn from this comrade and add an extra brick to socialist construction."

76. Everyone on the building site at once responded to this, digging and lifting with great energy. The bricklayers could hardly keep up and people could be heard crying, "Put twenty more on mine!" "I'll take twenty more!" The loudspeaker came on again to say, "Comrades, here is some good news for everyone. Although it is two hours before the shifts change, the transport group has already finished its work for the entire shift."

77. When the old man at the equipment depot heard the loudspeaker, he was delighted, for he had just discovered Wang Da-li's letter which had fallen out of Lei Feng's jacket and he thought it was Lei Feng's. So he quietly copied out the name and address of the sender to give to the broadcaster so that they could announce that it was in fact a P.L.A. comrade called Wang Da-li.

78. In order to get back to the squad on time, Lei Feng had to return his barrow and collect his jacket from the old man, to whom he said, "I've returned the barrow and have come for my jacket. Thank you very much. Good-by!" The old man handed over the jacket and, smiling as he looked at Lei Feng, he thought to himself, "You weren't willing to tell me your name, but I know it."

79. When the head of the school heard the broadcast, he was also very impressed by the lofty Communist style of Lei Feng and he quickly hurried to the broadcasting post and asked Teacher Li to take him to the comrade from the P.L.A.

80. They hurried down to the transport group but could not find Lei Feng; so they asked the tall workman, "Where is that P.L.A. comrade?" The tall workman said, "When I came back with my barrow just now, I couldn't see him anywhere and I was looking for him myself. Presumably he has gone to return his barrow. Let's go and see if we can find him over by the depot." At this the three of them set off toward the depot.

81. The old man in charge of accounts handed over the piece of paper on which he had written Wang Da-li's name and address.

82. Having left the building site, Lei Feng posted Wang Da-li's letter and put Wu Kui's money in the bank and set out back to the squad.

83. Halfway back it began to rain, and as he was walking along in the rain he suddenly heard a small child crying. Concerned, he stopped and looked in the direction from which the noise came.

84. He saw an old woman, holding an umbrella in one hand and a bag over her arm. With her other hand she was leading a small child and she was obviously finding it difficult going in the rain.

85. Lei Feng quickly rushed up to the old lady and asked her where she was going. She replied that she was going to Zhu village to see her daughter. Since Zhu village was more than three miles from where they were and nightfall was approaching and the road was difficult, Lei Feng wondered how the old lady and the child were going to get there. He quickly said, "Old lady, I'm going in that direction myself. Let's go together."

86. So saying, Lei Feng took the child in his arms. The old lady was very pleased but she worriedly asked, "Comrade, is this really the way you are going?" Lei Feng replied, "Yes, it is—please don't doubt me. Let's go."

87. The child was still sniffling and so as he walked along with it in his arms, Lei Feng said, "Younger brother, don't cry. I'll sing you a song." So saying, he started singing the song which begins, "I'm a soldier from the ordinary people . . ." The child stopped crying and listened to Lei Feng singing.

88. The rain became heavier and the going became more and more difficult. They came to a river spanned by only a plank bridge. Lei Feng took the child on his shoulders and crossed in the river, supporting the old lady with one hand as she crossed on the plank.

89. Meanwhile the head of Wan Hua Street primary school, leading the workmen and teachers from the building site, came with a beating of gongs and drums to deliver a thank-you letter to Wang Da-li.

90. When Wang Da-li heard that they were looking for him, he came out to receive them. The head of the school shook his hand warmly and said, "Comrade Wang Da-li, we know that one of the P.L.A.'s greatest virtues is modesty but we cannot allow your contributions to the people to go unnoticed. You spent a whole day of voluntary labor on our building site and so now, on behalf of the school, I want to express our deepest thanks. . . ."

91. Wang Da-li was left quite speechless by these words of the head of the school. What on earth was he talking about? Wang knew perfectly well he had not been out of the squad room all day, nor had he taken part in voluntary labor. Realizing that there had been some mistake, he hurriedly said, "No, no, it was not me . . ." and ran back inside.

92. When the instructor heard the gongs and drums he quickly came out. Hearing what had happened from the head of the school and realizing that there must be some explanation, he invited the visitors into the company office.

93. Meanwhile Lei Feng had reached the end of Zhu village with the old lady and her child, and here where the path was steep and difficult, he had cleared away some of the undergrowth and mud and made steps up the slope for the old lady.

94. It was already dusk when Lei Feng saw the old lady and the child to her daughter's house. The child's mother opened the door to welcome them in and took the child and said, "It's pouring rain, how did you manage to get here?" The old lady said, "Before you say anything more, put on some hot water. I was lucky enough to meet a comrade from the P.L.A. on the road."

95. Lei Feng was soaked to the skin but as soon as he saw the old lady together with her family, he felt very pleased. He used the towel which she had given him to wipe the rain from his face and then hung it on a branch of a tree in the courtyard before quietly walking away. He frequently did good deeds like this and then, without saying a word, quietly left.

96. The mother of the child said, "Quickly, invite the P.L.A. man to sit down inside." The old lady called him to come in but there was no answer. Lei Feng had already long since departed. The old lady was very surprised and said, "He did not even cross the threshold or take a glass of water."

97. When Lei Feng got back to the barracks, it was already late at night and he stole into the dormitory. He had had nothing to eat all day and now for the first time he really began to feel weak and thirsty. He saw that someone had left a mug of tea on the table and he quickly gulped it down.

98. It was not clear who woke first, but a voice said, "Lei Feng is back," and at this all the soldiers got up. Some poured water for him to wash in, others asked him what had happened. Lei Feng said, "I had originally set off to see the doctor but as soon as I got outside, the air was so fresh and the surroundings so peaceful that the more I walked, the better I felt . . ."

99. Suddenly the lights went on and everyone turned to the door. It was the political instructor who had come in. Smiling faintly he said, "If you can't tell a lie, then don't lie!"

100. Lei Feng knew that this was directed at him and he quickly ran up to the instructor and said, "Instructor, you're not yet asleep!" The instructor said pointedly, "If someone is missing here, how could I possibly go to sleep?" Lei Feng, swallowing hard, said, "Yes, well, it happened like this . . ." The instructor took out the thank-you letter from the head of the school and said, "First you had better explain what this is all about."

101. Lei Feng had to acknowledge that he had taken part in the voluntary labor at the building site. The hot-tempered Wang Da-li could not contain himself and said bitterly, "Comrade Lei Feng, I have a criticism of you. Having done a good deed, why did you tell them it was me who did it so that they came beating gongs and drums to deliver the thank-you letter to me? Didn't you do this deliberately to make a fool out of me?"

102. At Wang Da-li's words, Lei Feng was dumbstruck. The instructor had already found out how the misunderstanding had arisen and when he explained to Wang Da-li how the old man had discovered Wang Da-li's letter, Wang Da-li said nothing more but he still felt far from satisfied.

103. As soon as Lei Feng heard the instructor's explanation, he immediately realized what had happened and said, "Ah, no wonder the old man gave me that strange look when I went to pick up my jacket from him!" Then he turned to Wang Da-li and said, "Comrade Wang Da-li, I really beg your pardon." Wang Da-li felt very confused and could think of nothing to say.

104. The instructor also asked Lei Feng what he had done after leaving the building site. Lei Feng then had to report how he had accompanied the old lady to her home. The instructor patted him on the shoulder and said, "Well done." Everybody was very surprised when they heard his story and said, "What a splendid fellow! Altogether he walked over seven miles out of his way." The instructor added, "Comrades, we should all learn from Comrade Lei Feng's spirit."

105. Lei Feng's lofty style of taking pleasure in helping others and not for a moment thinking of himself deeply affected every one of the soldiers, and in particular it was an excellent example for Wang Da-li, who, seeing that Lei Feng's clothes were soaked through, handed him his own.

106. At daybreak Wang Da-li felt extremely energetic and took up a broom and shouted, "Let's go and sweep out the courtyard." Lei Feng wanted to go too, but Wang Da-li held him back, saying, "Lei Feng, you ought to spend the day indoors, resting," Lei Feng said he was not tired and wanted to join the others and finish the sweeping before resting.

107. The instructor, however, also told him to stay behind and rest. After resting, he had something important to tell him. Lei Feng felt even less like resting on hearing this and he persuaded the instructor to tell him what it was. So the instructor said, "The Wan Hua Street primary school has invited you to become the outside instructor for the Young Pioneers to help bring up a Red successor generation. This is a glorious political task. Higher authorities have already given permission."

108. The Wan Hua Street primary school held a solemn meeting to welcome the outside instructor for the Young Pioneers, Lei Feng. The Young Pioneers of the whole school were sitting seriously in the newly built meeting hall and were eagerly looking at Lei Feng, who was sitting on the platform. They were saying to themselves, "Uncle Lei Feng, we are really going to follow your example!"

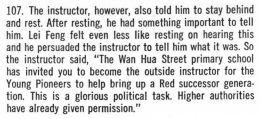

109. The head of the school warmly addressed the Young Pioneers, introducing Lei Feng. "Comrade Lei Feng was an outstanding tractor driver in his village and later, in the steel works at An-yang, he was three times chosen as an innovating worker, five times as a Red-Flag worker, and he was named a model worker eighteen times. Now he has become a Five-Good soldier in the Army. He is also a model soldier in economizing and an outstanding member of the Party. . . ."

110. The head of the school went on, "Comrades and students, we have already obtained his superiors' permission to invite Comrade Lei Feng to become the outside instructor for our Young Pioneers. Now we would like to extend a warm welcome to Comrade Lei Feng." The entire audience began to clap, and while they were clapping, the head of the school handed the official letter of invitation to Lei Feng.

111. There was more clapping as Zhou Da-qing, on behalf of all the other Pioneers, proudly tied the red scarf of the Young Pioneers around Lei Feng's neck.

112. On his way back to the squad Lei Feng thought to himself, "I'm going to make sure that this red scarf never loses its color and is never dirtied with the dust of bourgois thinking. One day there will come a time when the whole world will be as Red as this scarf and the children of the whole world will wear a scarf like this. This scarf is my Red starting point. I shall walk this Red road for the rest of my life."

113. Wang Da-li had decided to model himself on Lei Feng and one Sunday, taking advantage of the free time, he had quietly taken his comrade's dirty clothes and was washing them.

114. Lei Feng found him at it and, while thanking him warmly, began to wash an old pair of socks. Wang Da-li said, "Your old socks have been darned and repaired so many times you'll soon have patchwork socks. Don't they feel uncomfortable?" Lei Feng, however, replied, "As long as they don't interfere with my physical exercises or with my driving, I'll let them continue to serve me!"

115. The Young Pioneers were having their Pioneers' Day and had gone to plant trees beside a river. Lei Feng was glad to join in such a worthwhile task. The children were overjoyed when they saw their outside instructor working alongside them. Whatever the job, digging, planting, or watering, it seemed to go that much quicker.

116. Suddenly one of the children came across a broken screw in the earth, and Zhou Da-qing cried out, "It's an old screw! Let's throw it away!"

117. As soon as Lei Feng heard him say this, he quickly shouted, "Don't throw it away! You like hearing stories, don't you? Well, here's a story about a screw." At this the children quickly gathered around to hear.

118. "At one time," Lei Feng said, "I had just graduated from primary school and I was acting as a postman and errand boy for the district Party committee. One day I went with the district Party secretary down into the countryside and was looking at the busy rural scene without paying much attention to where I was walking, when I felt something under my foot. I slipped and fell and, when I climbed up to see what it was, found that it was a broken screw. I felt annoyed and kicked it aside . . ."

119. "The Party secretary immediately picked up the screw and wrapped it in his handkerchief. Then he told me to deliver a letter to the tractor station and, while there, to give the screw to the head of the station. Then he gave me some advice, saying 'If everybody in the country who came across a screw kicked it aside, just think how many would be kicked aside. But if everybody picked up what they found, think how much could be saved.'

120. When Lei Feng finished telling his story, he asked the children, "Children, think, in your own lives, how well do you pay attention to economizing, not wasting the smallest thing?" Zhou Da-qing then thought of how he had wanted to throw the screw away a moment before and, embarrassed, replied, "Uncle, I shall never forget for the rest of my life the story you have just told us and wherever I go I shall pay particular attention to saving things."

121. Meanwhile Wang Da-li received a letter from his family saying that there had been floods in his village and that his mother was ill and needed some money. At that moment he had no money on him and he was extremely worried. Wu Kui knew what was troubling him and said, "I sent all my money back to my mother but Lei Feng has some." Wang Da-li said, "Lei Feng lives such a hard life, it would be embarrassing to ask him."

122. Wu Kui found Lei Feng and told him what was on Wang Da-li's mind. On hearing about it, Lei Feng said to the Young Pioneers, "Children, I must go." And he quickly went to report to the political instructor.

123. That evening Lei Feng took out one of Chairman Mao's articles on caring for the livelihood of the people. He turned over and over in his mind Chairman Mao's instructions and thought of the difficulties of the people in the disaster area and the hardships of his comrade-in-arms Wang Da-li's family. His mind had already flown to the disaster area, so when the instructor came lightly into the room and stood behind him he didn't notice him.

124. Chairman Mao's works enabled Lei Feng to understand that the hardships of the people were his responsibility and that he should devote himself to helping them overcome their hardships. Now he realized what he ought to do and he wrote in his diary his warm emotion, "I saw the reports of flood disaster areas in Shen-yang in the newspapers, and Wang Da-li's family has also sent a letter saying their village is flooded and his mother is ill. I have studied the works of Chairman Mao and now I fully understand that the hardships of the people are my hardships and that it is my duty to help them overcome their hardships. I must spare no effort for the People's Commune and the people of the disaster area, and ..."

125. Having finished writing in his diary, he picked up the **Selected Works of Mao Ze-dong** again and planned to read further, but the instructor stretched forward and closed the book and said with concern, "It's long past lights-out. You ought to get some sleep. There's plenty to be done tomorrow."

126. On the following day Lei Feng and Wang Da-li received orders to take relief supplies to the disaster area. Just before they left the instructor said to them, "This truckload of supplies is sent to the people of the disaster area by all of the comrades in the regiment. You should have reached there by the afternoon in time to return by this evening. There is a further important mission for tomorrow!" Lei Feng and Wang Da-li replied in unison, "Yes, sir!"

127. The instructor then asked Wang Da-li, "Do you know why you have been made Lei Feng's co-driver this time?" Wang Da-li replied, "So that I can learn from Lei Feng in order to help the people of the disaster area." The political instructor said, "Not altogether! We have requested the superior authorities and received permission for you to take three days' leave to see if your family is all right." Wang Da-li was speechless with emotion.

128. The instructor was surprised. "What, aren't three days enough?" Wang Da-li burst out, "Instructor, the superior authorities are really . . ." The instructor realized what he was feeling and smiled. "All right, then, off with you now! Pay attention to safety!" Lei Feng and Wang Da-li saluted together and said, "We guarantee to accomplish the mission!" Then they boarded the truck and set off.

129. Halfway there Lei Feng saw a bus stopped at the side of the road with the passengers standing beside it. Guessing that something was wrong, he told Wang Da-li to look after the truck while he jumped down from the cab and ran back to the bus.

130. It turned out that one of the tires of the bus had been punctured and the driver was saying anxiously, "I don't know what to do! Here we are stuck in the middle of nowhere with the passengers stranded!" Lei Feng said enthusiastically, "If that's all it is, I've got a spare tire on the truck. Why not put that on?"

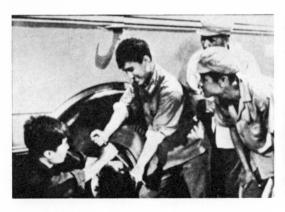

131. Then Lei Feng rolled over his spare tire and helped the driver put it on the bus wheel. The driver gratefully said, "Comrade, you are in the transport corps. How are we going to get this tire back to you?" Lei Feng quickly said, "Don't worry, I'll pick it up on my way back from the disaster area."

132. Once the wheel was fixed safely, Lei Feng turned to the passengers and said, "Old gentlemen, comrades, I'm sorry to have kept you waiting! Good-by!" The passengers were full of admiration for this excellent young soldier who delighted in helping others and were just about to ask his name, but Lei Feng had already boarded the truck and driven off.

133. Thanks to Lei Feng's help, the bus was now able to get on its way. The passengers all began discussing what had happened. One of the old peasants said, "It seems as if I've seen that comrade from the P.L.A. somewhere before. Ah yes, that's right! At the time of the New Year's festival he comes down to do voluntary labor on our commune. He's a good lad!"

134. Another passenger said, "Yes, I remember now, too! One time when I was going to Shen-yang, he was doing voluntary labor on the train, pouring out water for the passengers and sweeping the corridors. What a good soldier he is!" No matter where or when, Lei Feng always served the people. He had done many good deeds for many people but none knew his name.

135. As the truck was crossing a flooded river the engine went dead, and Lei Feng was unable to get it going no matter how many times he tried.

136. As always, taking upon himself the dirty work, Lei Feng refused to let his co-driver Wang Da-li get down from the truck and, taking off his shoes and socks and rolling up his trousers, took a starting handle and stepped down into the water to try to start the motor by cranking it.

137. When the motor was started, Lei Feng got back into the cab and wrapped the socks which he had just taken off into a bundle. Trying to persuade Lei Feng again, Wang Da-li said, "Lei Feng, it's not that you are short of cash. Why do you have to torture yourself like this? Surely you don't like having uncomfortable feet?" Lei Feng gravely replied, "These are much better than the bare feet I had when I used to go out on the mountainside to cut wood when I was a child."

138. Wang Da-li then took out a pair of new socks from his knapsack and handed them to Lei Feng, saying, "I bought these specially for you." Lei Feng tactfully refused by saying, "Keep them for me until every comrade in the squad has become a Five-Good soldier and then I'll certainly wear them." Wang Da-li could do nothing but take back the new socks and put them in his knapsack.

139. The truck arrived on time at the disaster area control headquarters, and, having seen the suffering of the people in the disaster area, Lei Feng and Wang Da-li, without paying any attention to their own exhaustion after the long journey, gave a hand with the unloading of the supplies. When the director of the disaster control center saw them, he quickly said, "You've had enough trouble getting here! Leave that and come inside and have some tea."

140. Director Liang warmly welcomed Lei Feng and Wang Da-li and poured them some tea and said, "Wherever there is trouble, you'll be there. The People's Liberation Army works together with us like hand and glove. When you return to your squad, please express these sentiments to everyone there." Just as he was saying this, a shout came from the next room calling him to take an urgent telephone message.

141. Director Liang took the message in the next room. It was about the serious developments in the flooding of Wang family village, which was Wang Da-li's own village, and Wang Da-li started to get very impatient. Lei Feng realized the reason and said, "Wang Da-li, go off now, quickly. Give my best regards to your mother." Wang Da-li then dashed off.

142. Not wishing to waste any more time, Lei Feng wanted to go back to the squad then and there, and, seeing that the room was empty, he took out a letter which he had already prepared and put it on the table and quietly left.

143. After Lei Feng had left the room, the director's assistant found the letter and handed it to Director Liang. He opened it and found a hundred **yuan** inside and written on the outside the words, "A contribution for the people of the disaster area," with the donor's name given as, "A People's Liberation Army soldier." He immediately guessed that it had been left by the two soldiers who had just departed and he quickly ran after them.

144. Lei Feng was just getting into the truck when Director Liang called him to a halt and asked him if the money was his. Lei Feng had to admit that it was. At this Director Liang said with great sincerity, "Comrade, we can accept your sympathy for the people of the disaster area but we cannot accept this money. You only get six **yuan** a month; to save one hundred **yuan** is no easy matter. You keep it for yourself, or if you don't want it, send it to your family."

145. As soon as he mentioned the word "family," the smile disappeared from Lei Feng's face and Director Liang quickly asked, "What, have you no family?" The sad expression left Lei Feng's face as he firmly replied, "No, I have a family; the Party and Chairman Mao are my new father and mother, the People's Commune is my family. Now my family here is suffering from a disaster and I have orders, and it is also my duty to come and help them. Director, you must accept this money."

146. Just at this moment the director's assistant found a paper packet and said to the director, "I've just found this on the ground." The packet contained Lei Feng's old socks which Wang Da-li, taking advantage of Lei Feng's absence, had exchanged for the new ones, but had dropped in his hurry.

147. As soon as Director Liang opened the packet, Lei Feng leapt forward saying, "Director, those are mine; please give them to me!" Director Liang said with emotion, "You yourself are wearing socks like these and you have contributed a hundred **yuan!** This makes it all the more impossible to take your money." Lei Feng said with great sincerity, "Director Liang, how can parents refuse a small token of their own son's inner feelings?"

148. Director Liang was deeply moved and said solemnly, "All right, we will accept the hundred **yuan** and I would request you also to give us this pair of socks. This is not only one hundred **yuan** and a pair of well-darned socks but an immense spiritual treasure. I myself am an old soldier and I am extremely proud that there is a successor generation like yourself!"

149. Lei Feng said, "Director Liang, I must get back to my squad now. Good-by!" He saluted everybody, turned, and jumped into the truck.

150. Everybody was very impressed by Lei Feng's modest and simple life-style and his selfless and generous attitude toward the collective and the people. Director Liang and the others waved to Lei Feng, obviously reluctant to see him go, and called after him again and again, "Good-by, good-by!"

151. Lei Feng waved good-by to them all and then, feeling very happy, started off.

152. Meanwhile, that evening Wang Da-li reached his village. It was already dark and he could see the lights flashing on the dikes around the village and could hear the shouts of people fighting back the flood. He followed the flooded road into the village and ran toward his home.

153. He found his mother busy at home making red paper flowers and asked, "Mother, why aren't you resting? Why are you doing this?" She replied, "This afternoon, at a crucial point in fighting the flood, several people did particularly well and the flood was successfully brought under control. Tomorrow the commune is holding a congratulatory meeting and I wanted to contribute something, so I am making these flowers." She felt very happy to see her son back and busily started to prepare some food for him.

154. As Wang Da-li was eating, he asked after her health and she said with a smile, "I'm all better now. Thanks to the care of the commune and thanks to your thoughtfulness, I've no longer anything to worry about. As soon as I received that twenty **yuan** from you, my illness was cured by half." Wang Da-li was quite speechless with surprise and said puzzled, "I didn't send any money!"

155. His mother was also puzzled, so she quickly fetched the letter from a drawer and handed it to him, saying, "You see, here's the letter!" Wang Da-li quickly took the letter. One glance was enough for him to understand.

156. "Dear Mother,
I have received your letter with the news of the flood in the village and your own illness. Please accept the twenty **yuan** which I am sending in this letter,
Your son."

This intimate note had been written by his own comrade-in-arms, Lei Feng! Lei Feng had taken his comrade-in-arms' mother as his own and had taken his comrade's troubles as his own. Once again he had quietly done a good deed.

157. Wang Da-li told his mother that the money had been sent by one of the soldiers in the squad, Lei Feng. With great feeling his mother said, "Lei Feng! What a splendid child! Your mother would really like to meet him!" As she said this tears came to her eyes.

158. Inspired by Lei Feng's class friendship, Wang Da-li forgot his tiredness and opened the door to go out, saying to his mother, who asked him where he was going, "I'm going to the dikes to help fight the flood!" And with this he dashed off.

159. He worked until dawn, and when he got back home he told his mother that he was returning to the squad. His mother said, "As soon as you came home you went out to fight the flood. Why don't you have a rest for a while before rushing off again?" Wang Da-li replied, "Mother, my superiors gave me leave so that I could come and see how you were, and now that I find you've recovered and the flood-dikes are well built up, there is nothing for me to do here. That's why I'm returning to the squad before the leave is up."

160. Remembering that the political instructor had said that there was an important task to be done that day, Wang Da-li wanted to return as quickly as possible to go out again in the truck with Lei Feng. So he ran all the way to the long-distance bus terminal.

161. When he arrived at the bus terminal the passengers were already beginning to board the bus. The woman in the queue ahead of Wang Da-li suddenly discovered that she had dropped her ticket and was in something of a panic. The ticket collector tried to calm her by saying, "Auntie, don't worry! Try and remember where you dropped it." The woman said she'd looked everywhere but could not find it. Wang Da-li thought of Lei Feng's acts of taking pleasure in helping others and he deliberately set about following Lei Feng's example.

162. He heard that the woman was going to the Zhang family village, so he quickly went to the ticket office and bought a ticket for her.

163. Wang Da-li then gave the ticket to the woman saying, "Auntie, I found your ticket; you can get on the bus now." The woman took the ticket, but not knowing the real circumstances, she thought that Wang Da-li really had found her original ticket. She thanked him warmly.

164. The ticket collector did not realize what had happened either, but thought that Wang Da-li had gone to search for a ticket belonging to a member of the masses and had done a good deed. Wishing to let people know of his good example, she asked him, "Comrade, what is your unit and what is your name?" Wang Da-li replied with one brief sentence: "I am a soldier of the People's Liberation Army!" Then he boarded the bus.

165. Wang Da-li got off the bus and then changed to a train. On the train too he set about helping the masses, especially old people. While he was doing this, there were two people reading the paper near him. One said, "Lei Feng! What a pity!" The other said, "He can't have been an ordinary person; his actions take up a whole page."

166. When Wang Da-li heard the name Lei Feng he pricked up his ears and quickly went over to read the newspaper. One look and he felt a wrench of anguish.

167. The paper, under the headline A SOLDIER WHO WILL LIVE FOREVER—LEI FENG, reported the news that Lei Feng had sacrificed his life for the public good and it gave the details of his life.

168. What a terribly sad piece of news! Wang Da-li would never have thought that his comrade-in-arms, whom he had seen only the day before, should today have taken leave of him forever. From this time on he would never again be able to live with him, to study with him, or to fight with him. He felt immensely sad and his tears flowed freely.

169. In order to commemorate and spread the revolutionary spirit of Comrade Lei Feng, the squad in which he had been a member while still alive received the honor of being named "Lei Feng Squad." And on that day the commander of the regiment presented the gloriously named embroidered banner collectively to the members of Lei Feng's squad.

170. The political instructor, his heart filled with a heavy sadness, representing the entire company, received the brilliant banner. They would all continue to tread the road that Lei Feng had trod and see to it that Lei Feng's spirit was spread throughout the company.

171. The head of the regiment also took the rifle which Lei Feng had used and presented it to Da Cu, who quietly received it, while promising in his heart, "I shall hold fast to Lei Feng's gun. I shall study Comrade Lei Feng's proletarian standpoint for distinguishing love from hatred and I shall firmly guard the socialist fatherland!"

172. The commander of the regiment also took the red scarf which Lei Feng had worn as outside instructor for the Young Pioneers and presented it to Wu Kui, whom he asked to take over this work of Lei Feng's and to cultivate Red blooms for the fatherland.

173. Finally, the commander of the regiment took Lei Feng's much-studied copy of the **Selected Works of Mao Ze-dong** and, with a look that expressed his confidence in him, presented it to Wang Da-li. Wang Da-li returned the commander of the regiment's look with a clear gaze which seemed to say, "I will certainly study the works of Chairman Mao as conscientiously as Lei Feng and really master the thoughts of Chairman Mao and become a Lei Feng style red member of the successor generation!"

174. From that time on, Wang Da-li studied hard the works of Chairman Mao just like Lei Feng. He too studied them wherever he went, and he determinedly armed himself with the thoughts of Chairman Mao, put a high demand upon himself, tested himself, and with all his heart and all his mind served the people and fought for the cause of the proletariat of the whole world!

175. Today more and more people are studying hard the works of Chairman Mao like Lei Feng, and there is a high tide of studying the works of Chairman Mao in the People's Liberation Army which, with real actions, answers the call of Chairman Mao and the Party to commemorate and study the magnificent Communist soldier Lei Feng.

176. The officers and men of the People's Liberation Army promise the Party to take Comrade Lei Feng as a model and study the works of Chairman Mao every day; do as Chairman Mao says; follow his instructions; and be a good soldier of Chairman Mao's.

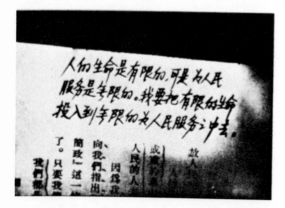

177. Although Lei Feng's life is over, his spirit continues to shine forth undiminished. Rivers have their source, trees their roots; the source and the roots of Lei Feng's spirit lie in Mao Ze-dong's thought and in the Party's directions. Let us forever remember Comrade Lei Feng's promises: to study for the people, to serve the people, and to fight for the people to the end!